THE PERSONALITY
OF CHRIST

BY
ABBOT ANSCAR VONIER, O.S.B.

FIFTH IMPRESSION

Cum librum cui titulus ' The Personality of Christ '
a Rmo P. Anschario Vonier, Abbate Congregationis
Nostrae, anglico sermone exaratum, Rmus P. Abbas
Thomas. Bergh, Censor a Nobis deputatus, recognoverit
et in lucem edi posse probaverit, facultatem facimus
ut typis mandetur, si iis ad quos pertinet ita videbitur.

Datum Sublaci in Protocoenobio S. Scholasticae, V.,
die 26 Junii 1914.

D. MAURUS M. SERAFINI, O.S.B.,
Abb. Gen.

D. ISIDORUS M. SAIN, O.S.B.,
a Secretis.

NIHIL OBSTAT.
Francis. M. Canon Wyndham,
Censor Deputatus.

IMPRIMATUR.
Edm. Canon Surmont,
Vic. Gen.

WESTMONASTERII,
die 26 Augusti, 1914.

Printing Statement:

Due to the very old age and scarcity of this book, many of the pages may be hard to read due to the blurring of the original text, possible missing pages, missing text and other issues beyond our control.

Because this is such an important and rare work, we believe it is best to reproduce this book regardless of its original condition.

Thank you for your understanding.

FOREWORD

THE four Gospels are the books most written about and most commented on in our own days. No age has produced anything superior, in finished scholarship, to the Gospel literature of our times. Even those exegetes from whom the fulness of the Christian faith is not to be expected are mostly reverent and often exhibit learning of the highest quality. Indeed, the modern system of 'Meditation,' on the other hand, as an integral part of spiritual and ascetical life, has produced an endless variety of books in which Christ's Life is set forth in a way that ought to be most efficacious in making us understand the Gospels, as they are ransacked by the writers of 'Meditations' in order to compel us to more intimate love for, and more close imitation of, Christ. Some of those productions are really superior studies of the wonderful character of Christ, and they give us what mere exegetical learning could never give—an insight into Christ's intimate Life. The present work is neither exegetical, nor apologetical, nor devotional, but strictly theological. Catholic Christology has received less attention from the public, though our own days have seen the production of some first-rate treatises *de Verbo Incarnato* by professional theologians. Yet we cannot entirely neglect the theological view of Christ without grave dangers to both our exegetical and devotional efforts. In my own humble way I am trying to help in filling up the great gap with the present modest book.

The English Fathers of the Dominican Order are bringing out an English translation of the third part of the Summa of St. Thomas Aquinas, which is his treatise on the Incarnation. That there should be a demand for such a work, in the Anglo-Saxon world, is a thing to rejoice the Angels; there are evidently men amongst us eager to penetrate the subtleties and sound the depths of the masterpieces of religious thought.

My book is a very unconventional rendering of the most important points of the third part of the Summa; but I trust that I have at least succeeded in giving the spirit of the great medieval saint and thinker, and if the following pages produce a desire in the reader to go to the Summa itself, I shall consider that I have had a notable success.

ANSCAR VONIER, O.S.B.

BUCKFAST ABBEY.
May 1, 1914.

CONTENTS

CHAPTER		PAGE
I.	THE METAPHYSICS OF THE INCARNATION .	1
II.	THE CHRIST OF THE GOSPELS, OF CHRISTIAN THEOLOGY, AND OF CHRISTIAN EXPERIENCE	8
III.	CHRIST AND THE SCIENCE OF COMPARATIVE RELIGION	14
IV.	CHRIST THE WONDERFUL	20
V.	AN ATTEMPT AT DEFINING PERSONALITY .	29
VI.	THE REPLACEMENT OF HUMAN PERSONALITY BY DIVINE PERSONALITY . . .	39
VII.	THE CONTINUANCE OF THE HUMAN NATURE IN CHRIST	45
VIII.	'AMEN, AMEN, I SAY TO YOU, BEFORE ABRAHAM WAS MADE, I AM' . .	48
IX.	HOW COMPLETELY CHRIST'S HUMAN NATURE IS DIVINE	53
X.	THE WORD WAS MADE FLESH . . .	60
XI.	A SCHOLASTIC HYPOTHESIS . . .	64
XII.	'INSTRUMENTUM CONJUNCTUM DIVINITATIS'	69
XIII.	THE AIM OF HYPOSTATIC UNION . .	85
XIV.	THE TWO WILLS AND THE TWO OPERATIONS IN CHRIST	90
XV.	CHRIST'S KNOWLEDGE	95
XVI.	IN CHRIST	108
XVII.	CHRIST ALL IN ALL	112

CONTENTS

CHAPTER		PAGE
XVIII.	Christ's Reserves	122
XIX.	The Hiding of Christ's Godhead	128
XX.	The Form of the Slave	132
XXI.	The Transition	142
XXII.	Christ's Sincerity	152
XXIII.	The Great Life	161
XXIV.	God Meeting God	176
XXV.	The Man of Sorrows	181
XXVI.	The Happiness of Christ	185
XXVII.	Christ the Strong One	190
XXVIII.	The Misunderstandings of the Gospel	196
XXIX.	The Christ Tragedy	202
XXX.	The Character of Christ	210
XXXI.	Christ's Place in the World	221
XXXII.	Christ and the World's Progress	230
XXXIII.	The Power of Christ	235
XXXIV.	The Finding of Christ	238
XXXV.	Christ the Father of the World to Come	242
XXXVI.	The Link between Christ's Mortal Life and the Eucharist	247
XXXVII.	The Majesty of the Eucharistic Presence	251
XXXVIII.	The Blood of Christ	255
XXXIX.	The Optimism of the Incarnation	260
XL.	Christ the Hero	268
	Conclusion	271

THE PERSONALITY OF CHRIST

CHAPTER I

THE METAPHYSICS OF THE INCARNATION

THERE is from the very beginning of our Lord's earthly life the substitution of the personal element for the purely legal element. He is a mysterious personality, and the whole success of His religion lies in His being trusted, in His being followed, in His being understood; the main precept of His religion is a personal precept of love for one another. In other words, instead of material legal observances He established the great observances of the human heart, of mutual understanding, of mutual support, of mutual love. 'Bear ye one another's burdens, and so you shall fulfil the law of Christ.'[1]

It is the triumph of His grace to keep human beings in the oneness of religious faith without imposing upon them any strict obligation of

[1] Gal. vi. 2.

uniformity in external ascetical practice. He Himself, in His own Person, is the unifying force of Christianity. His first disciples followed Him in the simplicity of their new friendship, carried away by His ineffable charm. No doubt they gloried in being the followers of so great a rabbi, and yet they had no external observance to make them into a school. How could they be the followers of a teacher without fasting, whilst the disciples of John and the disciples of the Pharisees fast so frequently? In other words, how could any man be a disciple of another man unless he carried in himself the badge of that man's mastery in the way of a fast, or an ablution, or a prayer?

Men hold their fellow men together with the chains of some external austerity; no man can be another man's master in truth and reality without putting upon the neck of the disciple the iron yoke of bodily observance; yet it was to be the achievement of the new rabbi to have a school whose only observance it was to believe and to have confidence in Him, and to have friendship and love one with another. 'By this shall men know that you are my disciples, if you have love one for another.'[1] 'Can the children of the marriage fast as long as the bridegroom is with them? . . . But the days will come, when the bridegroom is taken away from them, and then

[1] St. John xiii. 35.

METAPHYSICS OF THE INCARNATION 3

they shall fast in those days.'[1] Fasting has its part in the formation of a Christian. But you are not Christ's disciple simply because you fast four times in the week, whilst John's disciples fast thrice, and the Pharisees twice. ' By this shall men know that you are my disciples, if you have love one for another.'

The early attraction to Christ and fidelity to Him have all the joyous liberty of a nuptial feast; attachment and fellowship are all the surer because the feast is bright and gay; serious work is to be done after the feast, but the memory of the feast remains the undying tie of attachment.

The peace and the prosperity of the Christian cause are all in that. All conversion, all sanctity, must be associated with Christ's Person and the human persons with whom our lot is cast. Sanctity may indeed have certain secondary variations. With some souls Christ's Person is the predominating element; with other souls, thoughts—active thoughts—are concerned more directly with the visible human persons; but persons it is, and Christian religion is in danger where legal observance of some sort begins to crowd out the personal element, when all spiritual efforts are directed towards the scrupulous carrying out of a system of observances for their own sake without a personal purpose.

[1] St. Mark ii. 19, 20.

The spirit of Christianity, despite its ascetic purity, is diametrically opposed to such a material conception of the ethical life, and the temporary successes it may obtain are but the harbingers of final catastrophe. It is our Lord's exclusive privilege to be Law, or better still to be a substitution for all law. The human mind is jealous of such a position because the human mind resents being bound to a person; but as our Lord's Person is a Divine Person, as it is the second Person of the Trinity, the jealousy of the human mind is not warranted in the case of Christ.

The Pharisees took umbrage at our Lord's Person much more than at His doctrine. Abstract laws or external observances never arouse hatred and jealousy, just as they do not arouse love and sympathy in the measure in which a person arouses those feelings.

The great theological doctrines therefore concerning our Lord's Person have an intimate connection with our Lord's spiritual position in the world, because our Lord is nothing if not a Personality. His Grace is nothing if not a grace of love and of mutual understanding. There is no profit from the Gospel unless it be the perfecting of the human mind and the human heart. A man may invent an ascetical system and find other men to submit to it, but no man can make of his own person the irrevocable voice of conscience, the all-satisfying food of heart and mind. Our Lord is the only Person who ever could.

No man can make of the relations of other men with their fellow men the badge of true discipleship; our Lord is the only exception, and no one questions His authority and right to do it. The teachings therefore of Christian theology about our Lord's Person ought to be of intense interest to every follower of Christ, and His being a Divine Person should fill us with unbounded joy.

The history of Christian sanctity shows in innumerable souls an intense personal love for Christ: such is the historical fact. The question may be asked whether such deep personal friendship with one that is not of this world would be at all possible if He were not a living Divine Personality. In other words, Is not the Personal Love of Christ such as history reveals it, a psychological proof of His Divine Reality?

One thing is certain: it does not exist elsewhere —the personalities of the non-Christian religions are not the elements of the human conscience such as Christ is.

It would be a great mistake, therefore, to think that what we might call the metaphysical truths of the Hypostatical Union are barren and unpractical verities; they are, on the contrary, indispensable to any rational explanation of our Lord's position with the human race. There is in Christ a kind of multiplicity of spiritual presence that makes Him the personal spiritual friend of millions of souls; He has a kind of universality of presence and action, which interferes in no way with the intense individuality of His relations with particular souls. Such is the Christ of experience and history. In His humanity He has for all practical purposes the illimitability of Divinity itself; He is truly the Universal Friend, and yet no one ever was such an exclusively personal friend to individual members of the human race.

Now, such intense individuality with such comprehensive universality has but one explanation: Hypostatic Union, or Divine Personality, the mystery of one human nature existing through God's personal existence. In our own days more than ever, philosophical minds dread the rule of a mere individual, however holy that individual may be. It does not seem as if an individual being could ever be such as to give satisfaction to the mind of a race. So we find constantly in modern theologies the substitution of the ideal for the individual. Such efforts at substitution are anything but blameworthy; it is certain that no merely human individual could ever furnish a complete ideal for mankind, could ever be a life-giving, practical ideal for the human race. But, on the other hand, modern theologies are quite wrong in applying that process of substitution to Christ;

there is no need of substituting an ideal Christ for the historic Christ, precisely because the Christ of the Gospels, the Christ of Catholic theology, possesses in truth and reality an infinitude of Personality. There is no limitation in Him. Without that infinitude of Personality, as far as the race is concerned, an ideal Christ would be indeed preferable to a concrete personal Christ.

This is why I say that the great metaphysical principles underlying Hypostatic Union are of immense practical import. I do not mean that individual souls do make those great truths a practical study ; they simply possess Christ, and are happy in the possession. But for the philosophical mind that begins to consider Christ's position with mankind, the metaphysics of the Incarnation are indispensable.

CHAPTER II

THE CHRIST OF THE GOSPELS, OF CHRISTIAN THEOLOGY, AND OF CHRISTIAN EXPERIENCE

IT may be said of our Lord that His written life is far from being proportionate to His place in the world of souls. To a very great extent love for Christ is independent of the Gospels taken as mere narratives. In most cases, love for Christ exists in the human soul long before the books of the New Testament have been taken up as a spiritual study. Children of tender years will kiss a crucifix with the reverence of deepest love, because it is the image of Christ; and it would be an entire disregard of facts to say that the boy of six loves Christ so deeply because he has been made to understand the sublime charity of His Crucifixion from the gospel narrative. Long before the child is capable of understanding the great moral beauty of Christ's passion, he loves Christ crucified as sincerely as he loves his parents. A deeper comprehension of the love-drama of Christ's death is almost exclusively the achievement of more mature sanctity. Nor is this the peculiar characteristic of childhood's love for our Lord; the observation holds good much more generally. What there is of living faith in Christ in this world is out of all proportion to what there is written of Him, and, still more, to what practical perusal there is even of the written documents. For millions of men and women Christ is a great living Personality, dominating their innermost thoughts; yet with nearly all of them it is perfectly true to say that it is not the habitual perusal of the Gospels that has given to Him such a place in their soul. Their knowledge of the Gospel is not a very intimate one; they are satisfied with its general facts, whilst Christ Himself is a very clear, very distinct power in their life. If the study of our Lord's written life is made a special spiritual practice by a Christian, it is because the Gospel speaks to him of One whom he loves and knows already, just as the lover takes the keenest interest in being told of the doings and movements of the person loved.

It seems paradoxical, yet it is the experience of all observers of spiritual things: no one profits by the Gospels unless he be first in love with Christ. But this psychological fact may be stated in a yet more comprehensive form: The sacred Gospels are no adequate explanation of the place Christ holds in the hearts of men. They may account for the spiritual portrait of Christ which Christian men and women hold enshrined in their minds, but they do not account for the power with which Christ sways the hearts of millions. From time to time there are great Gospel enthusiasms passing over the Christian world. The sacred text is distributed broadcast in cheap editions; sayings of Christ are seen everywhere; even the very modern billposter is pressed into service to render Christ's sayings accessible to the man that runs. These manifestations of zeal, however laudable, are generally short-lived precisely because they never .succeed in stirring any deeper feeling.

Great nations in Europe live in the faith and love of Christ, and it may safely be asserted that any textual knowledge of our Lord's sayings is conspicuous by its absence in the vast majority of the good Christians of those nations. Christ for them is not a text, but a living Person, whose presence and whose look is infinitely more drastic in its spiritual effect than any saying of His recorded in the Gospels; and if the Gospel text is at times like the sword of fire to the soul, it is because it is connected with the living Presence, because it is read in the living love of Christ.

On the other hand, it is true again to say that the Christ of the human soul is not greater than the Christ of the Gospels. It is easy enough, for instance, to see what Christ was to the soul of St. Teresa, to the soul of St. Catherine. Those great mystics have left very clear records of their faith in and their love for Christ. Yet the ' Divine Master ' of St. Teresa's writings is not greater than the ' Master ' of the Gospels. St. Teresa did not create in her intense religious consciousness a Christ not warranted by the sober Gospel narrative. She may speak of the Spouse of her soul with greater enthusiasm than the Evangelist; but she never says a greater thing than was said by the Evangelist.

With Christ, the soberness of the narration belongs to the official historian who has lived with Him or His disciples. The enthusiasm is found in the ordinary worshipper to whom the work of the historian is more a canticle of love than a source of love. But the enthusiasm of the worshipper never assumes anything about Christ's merits which cannot be stated in the exact language of the Evangelist.

It has been said with great truth of certain religions that they are like inverted pyramids standing on their apex. The basis is the thinnest part, and the monument broadens as it leaves the almost invisible starting-point. The religious consciousness of the race has evolved a vast religious personality from a being of much smaller compass. Now, such a comparison would be quite unfair with the position of Christ in the world. The Christ of our Eucharistic Congresses is not greater than the Christ of St. John's Gospel. With Him there is no gradual broadening of a religious ideal, till it covers the whole extent of the human mind. The Christianity of the Gospels is as broad as the Christianity of the Summa of St. Thomas. But where the disproportion comes in is the efficacy and vividness of Christ's Personality as realised by human souls. No books, even divinely inspired, could create in the human consciousness such a presence of a living God-man, even if such books were constantly perused by the believer.

It is the conviction of all Christians that Christ enters into the secrets of their hearts, and that they are answerable to Him for their innermost thoughts. Christ is not only the object of their worship, He is also the voice of their conscience; and more than that, He is their Judge, He is the umpire of their eternal destiny. Here again it could not be said that Christian conscience has evolved a Christ not warranted by the authentic records of Christianity. We have endless utterances in the sacred Gospels and the Apostolic writings stating most clearly Christ's judicial powers. 'For neither doth the Father judge any man, but hath given all judgment to the Son.'[1]

It is the common teaching of theologians that there is in man a life that is inaccessible to the gaze even of the greatest spirits. God alone can read the secrets of the human heart; it is the most

[1] St. John v. 22.

incommunicable portion of our being; it is there that we show practically our individuality. The stronger the man or the woman, the less ready is he or she to reveal that inner self. Perhaps a man in his whole life finds only one other man to whom he opens the treasure-house of his thoughts, and it may even be asserted that most men go through life with their hearts sealed. Readiness to manifest one's innermost thoughts, unless it be to a mind entirely in sympathy with one's own and thoroughly trustworthy, is not a sign of manliness; it belongs to the superficial, to people who have no deep life of their own. Now it is into that portion of our life that Christ, the Son of God and the Son of Man, has penetrated, according to invariable Christian conviction. It is impossible for a Christian to doubt the universality of Christ's knowledge as to the secrets of our hearts. Are we not habitually convinced of Christ's human way of discerning the secrets of our hearts? For us it is essentially a human knowledge possessed in a human and created manner. To speak in metaphors, we know that every one of our thoughts falls into one of the scales of supreme justice, but the scales are Christ's human mind and human heart; the impression made on the scales is a human impression —a created factor. Such is the Christ of practical Christian experience.

CHAPTER III

CHRIST AND THE SCIENCE OF COMPARATIVE RELIGION

CHRIST'S Personality is all-important in the religion of Christ. ' Who is He ? ' and ' What is He ? ' are vital questions for Christianity. A religion outside the circle of that wonderful personality may be a most respectable system of morals and even of doctrines, but it is not Christianity. It would always be *Hamlet* without the Prince of Denmark. This English proverb is so telling that there is no profanity in using it in conjunction with the great drama of Christianity.

Christian religion can never be put on a par with other religious systems, simply because it is not a system but a Person. It cannot come under the scope of the science called ' Comparative Religion ' because its central facts—those facts that constitute its differentiation from the other religions of the world—are the manifestation of a divine genius of infinite originality. Comparative religion is a branch of human learning I revere deeply. I cannot conceive anything that could become more fascinating for the mind than to find out the parentage and relationship of the religious thoughts of mankind to their hundredth remove. But when all has been said, and everything has been compared, the fact remains that there is only one such being as Christ known to the religious world. Or more exactly, the 'Christ-idea,' such as it is found in the Gospels, in Christian theology and Christian conscience, is so deeply original that it defies all comparison. I say 'Christ-idea' instead of 'Christ' in order to remain within the scope of science. Science, being concerned with experiment and observation, can observe the Christ-idea in the world, as it is not a thing hidden under a bushel; it is seen everywhere in the world of to-day; it is the easiest of all tasks to find out from history what it was in the past.

Nothing could show more clearly this deep originality of the Christ-idea and its unique position in the world of religion than the great religious strifes within the Christian pale itself that filled, and are still filling, the world with their shrill echoes. Is it at all a thinkable situation that Mohammedans, for instance, should quarrel amongst themselves as to whether there were one or two persons in their prophet, or whether the divine person in him had absorbed the human person; whether there was a human will besides a divine will in him; whether there was the transubstantiation of bread into his body, etc.? . . . Yet Christians have taken, and are taking, sides in those very matters with a passion that comes from strong feeling on those subjects. Our very dissensions, therefore, make it evident that the Christ-idea has no parallel or term of comparison anywhere in the religions of the world.

The science of war, on land and on sea, is a definite science. Books are written on it, and mastered by young officers. But a Napoleon and a Nelson are not merely instances of a complete mastering of the science of war, they are war geniuses who make epochs, who make the very science of war to be different from what it was before them. Such personalities cannot come properly within the definitions of any war system. So Christ cannot be classed by the science of Comparative Religion because He is what He is in the religious world through His Personality. And as His Personality has such characteristics as cannot be found elsewhere, from the very nature of the subject, Christ is beyond all religious classification. Originality and classification exclude each other. Now, is there anything more deeply original than the Christ-idea? No doubt there is much in the practical Christian religion that resembles the tenets and practices of other religious forms. There is in mankind a vast store of religiousness, which is part of human nature itself, or it may be derived from more simple and more universal forms of piety such as there were in some remote and primitive state of human society. Then there is the natural expression of religious fear and awe, which is very analogous to the dread exhibited by the higher animals for their master. There are again certain subtle laws of the human spirit in its higher operations, which laws will act almost similarly, whether the ascetic be a Buddhist or a Christian monk. Thus, for instance, the effort of thought will make use of the same external means, whether the spiritual man be in Tibet or in Spain. But such things are merely the basic elements of all asceticism. They are the things that may be classified by the student and compared amongst themselves and pigeon-holed. Being found everywhere, they lack originality. But the moment Christ comes on the scene, there is evidently something quite new happening in the religious world.

If I may once more press into service my comparison of the war genius, the great soldier called Alexander or Napoleon fights with the old arms, with the time-honoured means of men, and horses, and weapons. Yet no man ever conquered as swiftly as Alexander, or struck as decisively as Napoleon. There is the old story of that martinet of an Austrian officer who maintained that Bonaparte was sure to be defeated because he did not follow the rules of war, such as the officer had learnt them in the military schools.

Christ wins the spiritual battle by making use of the old, well-worn spiritual weapons; but there never was a victory like His victory, because it consists in this, that He should 'draw all things unto Himself.' He establishes His Personality, and His success is complete then only, when men have begun to understand who He is and what He is. 'I have manifested Thy name to the men whom Thou hast given me out of the world: Thine they were, and to Me Thou gavest them; and they have kept Thy word. Now they have known that all things which Thou hast given Me are from Thee: because the words which Thou gavest me I have given to them; and they have received them, and have known in very deed that I came out from Thee, and they have believed that Thou didst send Me.' [1]

Spirituality is indeed indispensable to Christian sanctity; but the essence of Christian sanctity is a personal relation with Christ's Personality. Spirituality is a common possession of all mankind; it is mankind at its best, and therefore it is a necessary outfit for Christ's elect. At the same time there is a vast amount of genuine spirituality outside the Christian circle. I might say that even with the Christian soul its spirituality may

[1] St. John xvii. 6, 7, 8.

be at times greater than its essential Christian sanctity, as there is no practical or theoretical contradiction in the supposition that the effort after spiritual life, even with good men, may be many times greater than their efforts at entering into personal relation with Christ's Personality. I might say even that they are spiritual men rather than definitely Christian men, if we take the word 'Christian' to stand—as it ought to stand—for what is characteristically Christ's work. The practical realisation of the Christ-concept in the work of sanctity admits of infinite gradation even where there is Faith, and Hope, and Charity.

The Christian world is most prosperous, then, when it possesses its Christ most fully.

The principle of Christ's Personality once grasped changes one's spiritual life and lifts it up to a plane of wonderful supernaturalness. Spirituality itself may still be considered to be a common element. Life in Christ is the glorious secret of the new dispensation.

CHAPTER IV

CHRIST THE WONDERFUL

A GREAT deal of man's happiness comes from the power of admiration. To admire something is like a stream of fresh water flowing over the soul's surface; children are so happy because for them there is so much to wonder at. The deep solemnity of their untarnished eyes is the solemnity of wonderment. Woe to the man who has nothing to wonder at! his soul has lost all freshness, and his eyes are lustreless and vacant.

If at any time of our lives we cease to wonder, the fault must be all ours. The world in which God has placed man is an eternal wonder; admiration is the only thing which establishes a kind of equality and proportion between man and the vast world in which man lives. We do not understand the marvels of the universe. We see very little of the universe; we live, each one of us, in a very small corner of it; the universe is not ours, but it becomes ours through admiration— being so immensely greater than ourselves, we wonder at it, and our wonder grows as the immensity of the universe opens out more and more to the ripening intelligence. What we lose in proportion we gain in admiration, and we feel all the happier through our wonderment. It is the saddest thing in the world to have one's lot cast with people who have lost the gift of admiration. It is the cruellest and darkest captivity of the heart; it is external and internal darkness. It is the hardest purgatory of the soul; it would be hell itself but for the hope that the day will come that will set us free from the companionship of the unwondering souls, and place us amongst the spirits whose life is unending admiration. Let me be surrounded with the young and the infants, whose every movement and every sound is the expression of some wonderment, and I shall feel that my heart swells again with a happiness it has not known since childhood.

Christ the Son of God could never be man's eternal life if He were not man's eternal wonder. A Christ whom we could fully comprehend, whom we could understand through and through, could never be our life and our hope because we could not wonder at Him any more. It is an indispensable condition in all true and lasting admiration that the object of our admiration should always be greater than our knowledge of it, and that through the growth of knowledge, far from finding limits in the thing to be wondered at, we should be convinced more and more of the inaccessibility of those limits.

Love, no doubt, is born from knowledge and understanding; but short-lived and fragile would be the love which would be commensurate with knowledge and understanding. Love is best and strongest there where we know enough of a person to understand that there is in the person vastly more than we actually know. Every genuine and undying love lives not in the Holy of Holies, but merely in the Holy with its eyes fixed on the unapproachable Holy of Holies.

We find strong love for Christ the Son of God, a love that is as fresh as a spring morning, as unchanging as the eternal hills, only where there is the belief in Christ's divine nature, because then alone the created spirit has a scope for endless wonderment. Love dies when it finds a limit; limits are incompatible with love. If a good man's motive is explained to me, I shall wonder at his courage and unselfishness not so much on account of what he did, as on account of the character which the deed reveals. If I knew the man to be incapable of another such act, I could not love and admire him any more; in fact, my sentiment towards him is shaped much more by what I suppose him to possess than by what I saw him do. To make of Christ a human being is to deprive Him of the attribute of incomprehensibility; sooner or later we shall understand Him fully. Such theology would be the cruellest thing, as it kills in the soul the most life-giving element of all religion—wonderment that is always old and always new.

All admiration comes from depth. We admire what we know to be inexhaustible, unfathomable. It must be deep calling out to deep, if admiration is to be whole-hearted and overpowering.

Our Lord is indeed the Wonderful because in Him deep calls out to deep, because in Him there is a succession of spiritual regions, the one more beautiful than the other. Our Lord is not something simple, He is something very complex, something very deep, and it is only unhealthy minds that require a simple Christ, so simple indeed as to leave Him without grace and divinity. The first article of the Christian creed concerning our Lord's Sacred Person is this: He is one Person in two Natures. This duality of natures, so indispensable to Christian theology, is the great wonder, is the thing that makes Christ wonderful, because through that duality deep calls out to deep. There is in Him a human nature full of grace and truth; but when that human nature is searched into, it gives at once evidence of something deeper still—the divine nature. But this duality is merely the shortest possible expression for multiplicities of beauty which Catholic theology has undertaken to describe. Our Lord has all the perfections of man, He has the perfections of Divinity itself, and He has a perfection which is all His own—something between angelic perfection and Divinity. Those gradations of perfection, I repeat, unhealthy minds reject as burdensome; they crave for a simple Christ, but the simplicity they crave for is more the characterless transparency of common glass than the wonderful power of the hard diamond with its innumerable facets and its scintillating multiplicity. This gradation of perfections in our Lord's Person, so noticeable in Catholic theology on our Lord, is what makes Him so wonderful, because it is deep calling out to deep; or, to change the metaphor, it is mountains rising up higher and higher, and when you have reached one summit you find yourself at the foot of another giant amongst the mountains. So we find in practice that the most innocent and most loving of Christ's faithful revel in the theology of Christ's duality of natures, because a simple and loving follower is a born admirer, and his only fear is lest perchance a day might come when he could not admire any more. In this spirit then let us try to understand the wonderful multiplicity of Christ's perfections such as it is taught by Catholic theology.

In following the teachings of Catholic theology concerning our Lord's Person we are like the explorer whose mission it is to find out the course of a river. There are two ways of doing it. Sailing first for days on the endless expanse of the ocean, he comes to the mouth of some mighty Amazon, where it is difficult for a long time to distinguish the river from the ocean. Up he sails towards the river's source, borne onward by the inflowing tide as it contends for mastery with the current. After many days of journeying the river will lose to him its individuality; it is not one, but many rivers he has to explore; it is the watershed he is interested in more than in the individual river. Or, if the traveller chooses, he may begin his expedition on the mountain-top, follow one course, go down with it to the main stream, sailing down the main stream in the consciousness that sooner or later he will find himself entering the boundless ocean. There is a particular joy in the anticipation that the stream that carries him will become a limitless sea.

This second way of exploring would be more conducive to admiration than the first, because a traveller thus progressing from the mountain spring towards the ocean, passes from marvel unto marvel till all the marvels are merged in the marvellous ocean. This last simile represents the natural mode for man to find out the marvels of the Son of God. There is first His external human life; it is the mountain stream, fresh, powerful, of heavenly transparency, running in the deep ravines of His human sufferings. This mountain stream of the mortal life is absorbed by His spiritual life, His sanctifying grace, His angelic perfections of intellect, His glorified body; this again, vast and infinite though it be, is absorbed finally by a much greater infinitude—the infinitude of His Divinity.

St. Thomas acts not as the second but as the first explorer: he begins from the ocean, the Divinity, and follows up the great system of waters to the human sources of Christ's life. A glance at the disposition of the questions and articles in the third part of the Summa shows clearly the movements of this great theological explorer. He begins with Hypostatic Union—the presence of the Infinite Godhead in Christ; then he speaks of Christ's sanctifying grace, of Christ's supernatural virtues. He speaks of Christ's grace as the head of the human race; he speaks of Christ's knowledge, angelic and human; he speaks of the human power of Christ's soul, of His prayer, of His priesthood, of His adoption, of His predestination, of His adoration, of His mediation. It is still the main stream with the tidal movements of the ocean mixing with its waters and swelling them. Then he comes to the human life: Christ's virginal conception, His nativity, His baptism, His doctrine, His miracles, His passion, His death, His ascension, His resurrection.

I must crave the reader's indulgence for keeping his attention to the simile of a water-course. In order to be fully applicable to the present subject, instead of supposing a system of converging streams that come down from the mountain, we ought to suppose a system of streams flowing on level land so that the tides might come up to the very spring of the most humble brook. Nature has no such water system as far as I know; if it had, it would be a splendid illustration of a great mystery: the merely human actions of our Lord, besides flowing towards the infinitude of the Divinity, are constantly being swelled by the tidal movements of Divinity rushing along the channels of the human actions, and mixing with the waters of human sanctity. The stream that is a tidal stream has a double nature, so to speak: first there are the stream's own waters, and then there are the waters of the sea, carried along the native waters of the stream. So in the Wonderful there are many streams flowing into streams, but over them all there flow the waters of Divinity. No doubt it is this penetration of Divinity into every human act of Christ that compelled St. Thomas to adopt the method of exploration from sea to land.

I shall adopt the same method here for the instruction of those for whom this little treatise is written; the devotional method, however, which is essentially the wondering method, begins with our Lord's human life, begins with the 'Hail, full of Grace' and from the Virgin Mother, the sweet daughter of David. Then it journeys to the Word who dwells in the bosom of the Father, going from sweetness unto sweetness. It is not the only instance where the theoretical presentment of heavenly things follows an opposite course to that of the practical realisation of those things.

CHAPTER V

AN ATTEMPT AT DEFINING PERSONALITY

THE word 'personality' is a word to conjure with in our own days. The power of personality is the theme of every good work of fiction as well as of every good biography. A theological writer is of all writers the one who might be seen biting his quill for long moments of embarrassment for lack of the proper word, as society has taken his word from him and given it a different meaning. The term 'personality' holds as great a place in theology as in literature, but the rôles it acts are vastly different. It is true that the more modern meaning of personality—a powerful individualistic character—is not unwelcome to a theologian, as his Christ is the most winsome of all persons; but he has a much older right to the term 'personality,' and in his attempt to explain Christ's attractiveness he has to delve down in the hidden mysteries of much more austere concepts, and personality is winsome because it is something so solid; and it is with this view of personality, as the austere foundation of being, that the theologian is primarily concerned.

Locke's definition, or rather description, of 'person' is as good as any other, outside the Aristotelian and scholastic sphere of thought. 'This being premised to find wherein personal identity consists, we must consider what person stands for. Which, I think is a thinking intelligent being, that has reason and reflection, and can consider itself as itself, the same thinking thing in different times and places ; which it does only by that consciousness which is inseparable from thinking, and as it seems to me, essential to it : it being impossible for anyone to perceive without perceiving that he does perceive.'[1]

With Locke, the orthodox theologian says ' that a person is (essentially) a thinking, intelligent being ; that has reason and reflection, and can consider itself, as itself, the same thinking thing in different times and places.' The scholastic applies a similar definition to Deity itself, to the pure angelic spirit and to man. Yet, to the scholastic mind, Locke's definition of a person is not adequate. The scholastic asks with Locke why is it that a thinking being can think of itself, as itself, and it is his answer to that question that shows in him the deeper metaphysician. The English philosopher says that a thinking being thinks of itself, as itself, ' by that consciousness which is inseparable from thinking.'

Locke makes consciousness the reason of self-

[1] Locke on Human Understanding, book ii. c. 27.

ATTEMPT AT DEFINING PERSONALITY 31

consciousness, which is evidently a tautology. It is as if I defined my power of running through that movement that makes me run. The scholastic, though defining a person a thinking being, with self-consciousness (' to consider itself as itself ' is another expression for self-consciousness), has a deeper underlying metaphysical element which saves him from Locke's tautology, and it is that deeper underlying element which is the cause, so to speak, that makes the individual person. Self-consciousness, deep and mysterious as it is, is not so deep and so mysterious as self-being. The first is merely a result of the second. Now, the scholastic maintains that self-being underlies self-consciousness, as the cause underlies its effect, and he says that a person is constituted primarily through self-being, through the fact of having one's being as an exclusive and total property.

We all know Tennyson's immortal verses describing the gradual formation of the individual self-consciousness.

> The baby new to earth and sky,
>   What time his tender palm is prest
>   Against the circle of the breast,
> Has never thought that ' this is I : '

> But as he grows he gathers much,
>   And learns the use of ' I,' and ' me,'
>   And finds ' I am not what I see,
> And other than the things I touch.'

> So rounds he to a separate mind,
>   From whence clear memory may begin,
>   As thro' the frame that binds him in
> His isolation grows defined.
>
> This use may lie in blood and breath,
>   Which else were fruitless of their due,
>   Had man to learn himself anew
> Beyond the second birth of Death.
>   *In Memoriam*, XLV.

Yet this very evolution of the thought of the isolated ' I ' supposes an isolated possession of existence at the start. Now it is that perfect appropriation of being by the ' I,' long before there is a conscious distinction of oneself from other beings, the scholastic considers as the thing that makes a person. Scholastics are divided amongst themselves how to explain such an exclusive appropriation of being. Such differences of opinion cannot detract from the metaphysical value of the main principle, that a person is radically and eternally *sui juris*, a rational being with rights, and responsibilities, and duties that can never be shifted on to some one else's shoulders. Personality means incommunicable appropriation for weal and for woe of one's deeds. The highest manifestation of personality is moral merit and moral demerit, the fact through which a free act of the rational will is so entirely the property of the rational agent that God Himself cannot be held responsible for it, in the last instance,

ATTEMPT AT DEFINING PERSONALITY

without contradicting Himself. Moral responsibility is well calculated to open out to us a view of the might of personality. Let us think for one moment that both highest bliss in heaven and profoundest misery in hell are states for a spirit which God Himself could not transfer to another spirit without injustice.

Self-consciousness—the pet metaphysical reality of modern philosophies—is not so deep and so permanent a thing as moral responsibility, that all-important factor of Christian philosophy. A man may be perfectly conscious of his doing a certain act without his being responsible for it, as there is the possibility of his not having been a free agent in the matter.

The fact of moral responsibility is the most immediate result of the element that makes a person. Moral responsibility is not that element itself, but it is its firstfruit—its direct result. In moral responsibility we show that we have our being in our own hand. How could I ever be made to answer eternally for an act of mine, if that act were not mine with the exclusion of every other moral or ethical partnership?

Self-consciousness is near the root of our being, but it is not the root yet, and there is even the possibility of the act of which I am conscious not being all my own act.

Moral responsibility is much nearer that root,

for it implies in the last instance an exclusion of every other created will in my act of will. But it is not the root yet, just as will is not the whole man, the whole spirit. It springs from the root, and the root itself is personality. For a person is essentially a rational being that has responsibility, or, anyhow, may acquire it in time.

Moral responsibility is to my mind the natural key to the mystery of personality.

It may be objected that moral responsibility is too theological a fact to be made into a starting-point for the quest of personality, chiefly moral responsibility that stretches into the next world. My answer is that I am writing a theological book, not a philosophical one, for people to whom moral responsibility, implied in the words 'merit' and 'guilt,' is an intellectual certainty.

Moral responsibility and self-consciousness almost seem to touch in the phenomenon of the consciousness of duty, of the conviction—intellectual if there ever was one—embodied in the notion: I ought. Yet the two things, though converging, are still different. Moral responsibility is a fact quite independent of inner consciousness, or rather we know that we have the merit as well as the guilt of our practical answers to the 'I ought' as we have followed the voice or have disobeyed it.

There is an old scholastic axiom, 'Actiones sunt suppositorum'—'Acts belong to the person.'

ATTEMPT AT DEFINING PERSONALITY

Nothing could be truer, if we bear in mind the mystery of personal responsibility for our deeds.

I should describe personality as that reality within the creature that makes the creature's acts to be entirely his acts, with their full responsibility—a responsibility stretching into eternity. It matters comparatively little how we explain that great appropriation of being that underlies responsibility. That it is a wonderful and potent reality is clear to all those who admit moral responsibility. That it is a reality that pervades and dominates our whole being is again manifest from the results of responsibility, which affects our whole life, for weal or for woe. It is necessarily what schoolmen call a 'substantial' reality, a reality that is not merely accidental but one that is co-extensive with the individual being itself.

Before leaving this chapter I must say a few more things in order to remove certain misgivings that might arise in our minds at the hearing of some expressions made use of here as, for instance, 'appropriation of being,' 'exclusive possession of being,' 'exclusive responsibility of one's moral acts.' Is it not the first rudiment of piety to believe firmly that our being is the property of God, from whom we have received it; that our good acts, chiefly of the higher, the supernatural order, are the doings of the Spirit of God within our own created will?

The answer to such difficulties will be a further illustration of the greatness of created personality. Nothing is truer than the fact that all our being comes from God, by creation. But God's creative power is, so to speak, at its best in the production of a being that is so complete as to have a responsibility all of its own, just as God has responsibility. Pantheism, which means emanation of things from God, as opposed to creation of things *ex nihilo*, is warded off most conclusively by that duality of responsibility. That God should be able to produce outside Himself a being whose very constitution brings about within itself a responsibility that may put it eternally into opposition to the God that created it is the greatest achievement of God's creative power. So likewise with the share of God's grace in our moral acts, both natural and supernatural. No amount of divine *influxus* will ever take away the fact that it is my own act. St. Thomas would say that the divine *influxus* is of such a nature as to make my act more mine than ever. Such is his constant answer to objections about the preservation of free will under the divine *influxus*. Just as God's creative act at its highest results in a personality distinct from Him, so God's elevating act—this is a good expression for the supernatural *influxus* of grace—results in a meritorious deed that is the free will's own glory.

I have said already that even amongst schoolmen there are accidental divergences of opinion as to the precise definition of that far-reaching element in the created being that makes for absolute duality between God and His rational creature, even when God fills His creature with the graces of His own Spirit.

The older philosophy takes a personality to be something entitatively static. The modern philosophies make it into something that is practically all dynamic.

The older philosophy has the great advantage over its modern sister that it does the one thing and omits not the other. It allows for all that love of life which is the characteristic of dynamic philosophy. The older philosophy grants all and every one of the transient phenomena of psychic life postulated by modern thought. But behind the phenomena of conscious life there are for the schoolmen the static and stable elements from which life with its endless variations flows, and which give it continuity and oneness.

Personality is one of those static elements; perhaps it is the principal static element; it is the centripetal power in our very complex individualities—centripetal precisely because it is static. Such stability is not only perfectly reconcilable with the perennial flow of our conscious psychic life; it is its salvation, just as the deep banks of a river keep the river from becoming a nondescript swamp. Or better still, personality, the static thing in man, is to consciousness, the dynamic thing in man, what the mighty mountain range is to the stream : in its soaring solitude and unbending solidity flows the winding stream with all the charm of its rippling motion and babbling song.

Before concluding the chapter I want to emphasise once more that the thing which I call moral responsibility is not personality itself, but that it is an element of personality, and in its brightest manifestation responsibility allows us a deep plunging peep into the abysmal mystery of personality.

CHAPTER VI

THE REPLACEMENT OF HUMAN PERSONALITY BY DIVINE PERSONALITY

IT is the oldest and truest expression of the philosophy of the Incarnation to say that in Christ there is no human personality, but that the human personality in Him has been 'replaced' by Divine Personality. The great struggles of orthodoxy against Nestorianism resulted in the adoption of this formula by the Church. Christ is a human individual nature, without a human personality; in Him the Divine Personality of the Word does the functions of the human personality, and it does infinitely more, as behoves a Divine Personality. The maintenance and reality of the one individual human nature, detached as it were from its congenital and native element of created personality, and endowed with Divine Personality, is another dogmatic result, brought about by the Church's long strife with Eutychianism and its various ramifications. The separability of personality from the individual rational nature by Divine Omnipotence, and its 'replacement' by a Divine Personality, must always be factors of Christian metaphysics, if our system of thought be such as to allow for Hypostatic Union.

Any sanctification, any unction of the Spirit, any supernatural grace that is not a substitution of human personality in Christ by the Personality of the Word, is not Incarnation, is not Hypostatic Union; it is merely one of the ordinary works of supernatural grace. There are no limits to the powers of the Holy Ghost, to the ways in which He may elevate the rational creature above its own plane to a similarity with God. But sanctifying grace carried to its millionth power could no more be Hypostatic Union than extreme cultivation of voice in me could be a training of my mathematical powers. Hypostatic Union is a marvel of a different order, though not so different as not to be found in the same rational being, as not to have certain secret affinities with it.

Hypostatic Union requires first of all the absence of a congenital element in the individual nature: its native created personality. All the other supernatural elevations, worked by the Holy Ghost, far from starting with the absence of some natural endowment, presuppose on the contrary every native perfection and responsibility.

The missing, or rather discarded created element, finite personality, is not elevated or glorified by the Holy Ghost, but it is 'replaced' directly by a reality of the same order but of infinite altitude, the Personality of the Word. The ideas contained in the terms 'elevation' and 'replacement' express well the mutual relation of ordinary sanctification, even of the highest order, and Hypostatic Union. The Holy Ghost elevates to a higher plane the existing realities of the rational creature in ordinary sanctification. In Hypostatic Union the Second Person of the Trinity takes the place of a created element that ought to be there under ordinary circumstances, but has been left out to give place to an infinitely adorable substitute.

Such replacement could never come about, in a creature, unless the replacing Personality were Infinitude itself.

First, infinite power is required to interfere in a created being with the element of personality, for only a God of infinite creative power could make a responsible personality exist outside Himself; personality is God's divinest work, and as He alone places it within the creature, He alone can give it a substitute.

Secondly, such replacement requires what I might call Infinitude of subtleness on the part of the Person, thus superseding inside an individual created nature its congenital personality.

Thirdly, there must be in the replacing Personality an Infinitude of personal worth, precontaining in its oneness all the created personal worth possible. By personal worth I mean here the worth that accrues to an individual rational nature from its privilege of being such and such a person, with respective rights and responsibilities that stretch into eternity. Now, our masters in theology are far from being blind to the fact that not to possess its native congenital personality would be to the rational nature an immense disadvantage, unless the substitute be not only infinite, but also such as to precontain in itself what it comes to replace.

Suppose it to be a metaphysical possibility that my personality might be replaced, say, by the personality of a high spirit, it would be doubtful whether I should be the gainer or the loser. A finite spirit could never replace within me a congenital, essential element of my being without my being less myself.

But with the second Person of the Trinity, in whom all things are as in their eternal prototype, Christ's humanity has acquired boundless riches of personal worth, though it be without a created personality. For Divine Personality is infinitely congenital to it. Nothing short of this replacement or substitution by Divine Personality of created personality will do justice to the traditional view of Christ, the Son of God. I make so bold as to say that Hypostatic Union, thus stated with

REPLACEMENT OF PERSONALITY

theological exactness, is indeed worthy of the admiration of the keenest intellect. The whole difficulty resolves itself into this question: Is it possible for Infinite Personality to do inside an individual created nature the function of finite personality?

It is in this, and in no other sense, that God is said to become man.

No doubt many minds, unacquainted with Christian theology, think of a transformation of Godhead into manhood when they hear the phrase, and they naturally revolt at it at once. Their mental recoil would be more than justified if incarnation were such a transformation.

But that the phrase should mean, as it does mean, that Divine Personality 'does duty' within a human nature, for a created personality they seem hardly to realise; yet it puts quite a different face on the matter.

Other theologies, still admitting an incarnation, at their best speak of a mere indwelling of Godhead in the Man Christ, an indwelling of indefinite character, and bristling with metaphysical difficulties, when one comes to probe it.

Catholic theology, the child of the great councils of the fourth, fifth, and sixth centuries, by adopting the 'replacement' of personality by Personality, whilst giving the link that unites Godhead and manhood in Christ—a link that is almost palpable—

has not burdened man's intellect with a revolting metaphysical novelty.

That there are within the human individuum separabilities, if not actual separations of realities, is practically admitted by every serious system of philosophy. No philosopher could dream of man as of a non-composite being. Our dogma goes, it is true, to the root-separabilities, and thinks of Deity as being capable of replacing certain created elements without there arising pantheistic results.

CHAPTER VII

THE CONTINUANCE OF THE HUMAN NATURE IN CHRIST

THE present chapter is written in order to explain how the concept of a Divine Person absorbing and replacing the individual human nature in Christ would be pantheistic, whilst there is no pantheism, but a most glorious assertion of God's 'personalness,' in the replacement of human personality by the Personality of the Word. It is the oldest and most sacred of Christian dogmas that with this mysterious substitution of personality, Christ's human nature is as entire and as intact as my own nature. He is as perfectly human as I am. His humanity has indeed been immensely elevated by every kind of supernatural grace, but it has not been replaced —nothing in it has been superseded. How an individual nature is a distinct reality from personality I have already explained. Therefore there remains the necessity of showing how the Incarnation could never be a substitution of nature without its giving rise to monstrous philosophical consequences, whilst there are no such alarming results with the substitution of personality.

Nature is essentially the stream of life, born in the mountain fastnesses. It is all movement, all activity, all consciousness. Modern philosophies, being essentially dynamic and phenomenalist, are nature philosophies; they are hardly ever personality philosophies; they only busy themselves with modes of acting, without bothering about modes of being, and in their own generation they have been wise enough. Now, the idea of a stream suggests to me a comparison, which I think very useful in this most abstruse matter. Engineering skill has replaced for many a stream, at least sectionally, its original banks with artificial banks. There is no end to the power of the engineer; if he be given time and money, he might replace the banks of the Rhine with a stone dyke from Switzerland down to the North Sea. But no engineer, with an empire to finance him, will ever replace the stream itself by one of his own invention. The birth of streams belongs to the unalterable cosmic laws. I must crave the reader's pardon for suggesting an analogy between man's mechanical achievements and this most spiritual subject, Hypostatic Union. But have we not a great authority to justify the use of similitudes? ' And with many such parables He spoke to them the word, according as they were able to hear.'[1]

[1] St. Mark iv. 33.

CONTINUANCE OF HUMAN NATURE 47

Let the stream stand for individual nature. That God should in His own Person be personality to it is like replacing the original banks of the river with a more durable one. But that Godhead should replace nature itself would mean that the river is no longer the river it was; it has lost its identity. It would not be a stream of life that comes from earthly sources; it would be simply an outflow of Divinity.

But to return to more exact thought, life cannot be replaced by a Higher Life; thought cannot be replaced by Higher Thought; consciousness cannot be replaced by Higher Consciousness: but life, and thought, and consciousness may be appropriated by a Higher Owner. The function of nature is to live; the function of personality is to own.

CHAPTER VIII

'AMEN, AMEN, I SAY TO YOU, BEFORE ABRAHAM WAS MADE, I AM.'[1]

THE text that I chose for the title of this chapter is one of the many passages of the Gospel narratives that show how even medieval theology, with all its high metaphysics of the Incarnation, never goes beyond the theology of the Evangelist himself. It may state the matter in terms different from those of the inspired writer, but it does not state anything beyond the inspired writer's expression.

The above text is quite clear; its authority is undoubted; the Jews saw the purport of Christ's solemn asseveration: He gave Himself the age of the Deity itself. They pick up stones to punish the blasphemy there and then.

The declaration of His having unchanging divine existence, implied in the words 'Before Abraham was made, I am,' was not, humanly speaking, directly intended by Christ, but was brought

[1] St. John viii. 58.

about by the allusion of the Jews to the death of Abraham and to Christ's comparative youth. It was the Jews, not Christ, who introduced the subject of Abraham. The unexpected turn the controversy took shows how clear to Christ's consciousness was the realisation of His own superiority to time and space. I now quote a casual remark of St. Thomas, which he makes in connection with something else, but which shows that the mind of the great theologian habitually moved in a sphere which I might call the sphere of St. John's Gospel. The doctrine contained in the remark is an intellectual consequence of the metaphysical principle laid down by St. Thomas for the understanding of the Hypostatic Union. Yet intellectual consequence though it be, it is a natural commentary on the Gospel text quoted above. 'Although the human nature in Christ be something new, nevertheless the personality of that human nature is not new, but eternal. And as the name "God" is predicated of the man (Christ) not in virtue of the human nature, but in virtue of the personality, it does not follow that in the Incarnation we introduce a new God. But such a consequence would follow, if the man (in Christ) had a created personality, as those who put two persons in Christ (Nestorians) would be compelled to speak.'[1] Before Abraham was made, Christ is, because eternal Personality

[1] Quest. 16, art. 2, ad 3 um.

has replaced created personality. The thing represented by the term 'is' belongs to personality. Christ had eternal Personality, therefore He *is* eternally.

Christ's human nature did not exist from eternity; it was formed in Mary's womb. But it exists in virtue of an eternal existence, the Divine Personality. Suppose a man had lost his eyes or his hand; suppose the eyeball or the hand to be restored to him by Divine Power—it is certain that the eye or the hand would be much younger than the man's main organism. At the same time the new members would share the age of the whole organism, as they share its general vitality and power of existence. This comparison is used by St. Thomas in order to express how there is oneness of being, oneness of existence, and therefore oneness of age in Christ's Personality, though there be in Him the human element inserted at a given period of history into the vitalities of Divine Personality.[1]

The seventeenth question, from which the comparison is taken, is what may be considered the sublimest height of the metaphysics of the Incarnation. It contains two articles, and the second article is the climax of speculative thought: 'Whether there be only one "to be" in Christ.' The answer is in the affirmative.

[1] Quest. 17, art. 2.

The replacement of personality which I have spoken of is the definition of Christian councils. It would be a sufficient formula to enable us to state the mystery. St. Thomas has drawn all his conclusions from that great ecclesiastical definition. All our views of Christ, all our love for Him, are not only modified by it, but actually born of it. But when St. Thomas begins to raise the question whether there is only one existence, one ' to be,' in Christ, he evidently dares a high thing, more than seemed to be originally authorised by the language of the councils. Yet an affirmative answer to the question is the only thing that does justice to words like those of the text : ' Amen, Amen, I say to you, Before Abraham was made, I am.' That human organism that speaks, IS, exists, has being in virtue of the existence that is Eternity itself, just as the miraculously restored eye lives in virtue of the life of the old organism. For St. Thomas, the conclusion that eternal existence is the existence of the nature formed in Mary's womb seems to offer no difficulties. He arrives at it as calmly as you arrive at the conclusion that you want food when you are hungry. Existence follows personality, he says ; for it is only a personality that makes a rational nature exist finally. Now, Christ's human nature has Divine Personality ; therefore it has Divine Existence. It is God, because it exists through God's existence. Such is the meaning of that wonderful second article of quest. 17. Its calmness is as surprising as its speculative sublimity. Like the Divine Master who thought it no profanation to utter the words, 'Before Abraham was born, I am,' in spite of the uproarious tumult it raised amongst the Pharisees, St. Thomas, the great master of theology, thinks it no exaggeration to say that Christ's humanity has the same existence with the eternal God. After all, it is a smaller truth than to say that it has the same personality with the eternal God.

CHAPTER IX

HOW COMPLETELY OUR LORD'S HUMAN NATURE IS DIVINE

ST. THOMAS (second question) asks himself this question: Is Hypostatic Union natural to Christ as man? One sees the meaning of his interrogation. We have said that Hypostatic Union is nothing else than the personal existence of the Word, being directly the existence of Christ's soul, and of Christ's body.

The question, then, of St. Thomas is this: How far is this union between Divine Personality and human nature natural to the human part of our Lord's Person?

First of all, it could not be natural in the sense of its flowing as it were from the human, the created part of Christ; a creature of whatever rank could never have in itself the power of such a union.

It all comes from above. There is, however, another point of view. Our Lord's human part never was without that divine existence; neither His soul nor His body existed even for one instant in an undivine way; and it is on that account that it may be said that Hypostatic Union is natural to Our Lord as man, because as man He never knew any other sort of existence. It does not seem to imply contradiction that an adult human personality should be at a given moment hypostatically united with a divine person. But in that case, Hypostatic Union could not be called natural, as it succeeded a created human personal existence, and the Mother of that hypostatically assumed human nature could not truly be called the Mother of God. Our Lady, on the contrary, is truly the Mother of God, because Her Child never existed otherwise than as the Son of God.

However, we have not exhausted the subject yet. There is one more way for our Lord's human nature to be naturally divine, more excellent than the mere fact of His never having been anything but divine. It is this. The mode of Our Lord's formation in the womb of His Blessed Mother was such that the result had to be human nature with divine existence. She conceived from the Holy Ghost, and conception from the Holy Ghost is necessarily the origin of a nature that must have divinity. So Our Lord as man is naturally God, because the way in which He was conceived admits of nothing else.

This is clearly expressed in the archangel's message to Our Lady. 'The Holy Ghost shall come upon thee, and the Power of the Most High shall overshadow thee, and therefore also the Holy that shall be born of thee shall be called the Son of God.' He shall be called the Son of God, precisely because the Holy Ghost will overshadow her, so that Our Lord as man is God, in virtue of his conception through the Holy Ghost.

It might be said therefore that in Hypostatic Union the human nature is as divine as divine can be, not only because it always has been divine, but it is divine because, through the laws of the conception, it had to be divine.

'The grace of the (Hypostatic) Union is natural to Him in His humanity according to a propriety of His Nativity, as He was thus conceived from the Holy Ghost, that one and the same person should be naturally the Son of God and the Son of Man.'[1]

We ought never to think of Christ's humanity as in any way separable from His Divinity, as prior to it, or as being the object of a predestination by itself. It was always divine, and according to St. Paul's energetic expression 'Christ Jesus ... being in the form of God, thought it not robbery to be equal with God.'[2] There seems to be no inherent contradiction in the supposition that a living, grown-up human person might be united with a divine person hypostatically at a given moment. Human personality, then, would be 'swallowed up' by Divine Personality. But such a union would

[1] Quest. 2, Art. 12.   [2] Phil. ii. 6.

differ in many things from the Hypostatic Union that is in Christ. The greatest difference, a difference which perhaps would constitute an infinite difference, would be this, that in such a supposition the human nature would not be divine by the very laws of its conception and birth.

The hypothesis would safeguard Hypostatic Union, but it would not be Christianity, and the mother of the privileged human being would not be the Mother of God ; she would be the mother of a man who became God, which is a totally different thing. The Church in her struggle with Nestorianism established the doctrine not only of the substitution of Divine Personality for human personality in Christ, but also the title of Mary to divine maternity, because her Son was conceived in such a wise as to be necessarily God.

In my hypothesis the man thus elevated to Hypostatic Union, though truly the Son of God, would owe endless gratitude to God for the favour. In the Hypostatic Union that is in Christ it could not be said that Christ's humanity owes a debt of gratitude for its privilege. It has Divine Personality, divine existence through the laws of its birth ; ' Propter proprietates Nativitatis ipsius,' as St. Thomas says in the article I have cited.

Nothing short of Hypostatic Conception can give us a complete idea of Christ. His flesh is all divine, and from the very beginning of the Nestorian controversies, the champions of orthodoxy appealed to the mystery of Christ's body in the Eucharist as an argument in favour of the personal union, from the very start, in Christ. ' This very fact that we acknowledge that the only begotten Son of God died in His flesh, rose and ascended into heaven, qualifies us for offering the unbloody sacrifice in the Church and, by participating in the holy flesh and precious blood of the Redeemer, for receiving the mystical blessing so as to be sanctified. We receive it not as a common flesh, nor as the flesh of an eminently sanctified man, or of one who has received dignity by being united with the Logos or by divine indwelling, but as the true life-giving and proper flesh of the Word. For since He is, as God is, in His own nature life, and is become One with His own flesh, so has He imparted to this flesh a life-giving power.'[1] This profession of faith, formulated in the council of Alexandria A.D. 430 under the presidency of St. Cyril, preparatory to the great Ephesine council, shows how clear and definite the views of Christian thinkers were as to the extent of Christ's divineness.

There is one more consideration that finds a natural place here : St. Thomas says[2] that Hypostatic Union is something created. This doctrine, strongly emphasised by Aquinas, whilst containing

---
[1] Hefele, *History of Councils*, iii. 30.
[2] Quest. 2, art. 7.

a world of wisdom, might be easily misleading, as implying apparently an inferiority of divineness for Christ's humanity.

That Hypostatic Union is a created thing ought to be clear to everyone, after a little thought. In Hypostatic Union Divine Personality replaces human personality; or, what is more to the present purpose, Divine Personality is united with an individual human nature. Now such a union is brought about by God's creative Omnipotence, uniting the two extremes into the One Ineffable. If creative Omnipotence did not intervene, a human nature could never have divine existence, Divine Personality, except in the pantheistic sense. Personal being outside God is always the result of a creative act of God. Now the circumstance that personal being exists before—namely, the second Person of the Trinity—does not alter the case. It had to be given to an individual human nature, and such granting, or such uniting, supposes as much a creative act as the production of personal being *ex nihilo*. In this sense Hypostatic Union is something created, *aliquid creatum*. It is the result of a created act, but a result that implies a series of infinitudes. For though Hypostatic Union be something created, in no sense is it something finite. To be a created thing and to be a finite thing are not necessarily synonymous. Philosophers admit degrees in Infinitude: there are greater infinitudes and lesser infinitudes. In order to explain Hypostatic Union exhaustively, no doubt every kind of infinitude ought to be pressed into service : it is deep calling unto deep. But one thing is certain : it has no finite element, though it be a created marvel. Christ's human nature no doubt has finite elements, but that thing that makes the nature divine, Hypostatic Union, is all made up of Immensity and Illimitability.

CHAPTER X

THE WORD WAS MADE FLESH

THE commonest theological formula stating the Mystery of the Incarnation is this: 'God was made man.' We have scriptural authority for it in the words of St. John's Gospel, first chapter: 'And the Word was made flesh.'

St. Thomas makes an exhaustive study of the various formulas that express the wondrous mystery, in the sixteenth question of his third part of the Summa. It shows amongst other things how various were the aspects of the mystery known to the great thinker.

Now the formula 'God was made man' has his full approval. It is a true statement. His interpretation is this: 'God is said to have been made man, because a human nature began to have being through the personality of a divine nature that pre-exists from all eternity.'[1]

In other words, for God to become man is merely

[1] *Ad primum.*

THE WORD WAS MADE FLESH 61

the fact of a Divine Personality doing duty of personality for a particular human nature. Such office, Divine Personality did not exert from all eternity, but started it in time, in the hour which had been predestined. So it is both orthodox and grammatical to say: 'God became man.'

Many of us would feel easier in our minds with that other formula, 'Man became God,' as it expresses better the elevation of human nature through Hypostatic Union, as it seems to contain no narrowing of the Godhead, but a broadening of manhood. Yet St. Thomas rejects the formula as misleading. His reasons are best given in the third article of the thirty-third question, where he treats of Christ's conception. I give his meaning. 'We say with great propriety of language that God became man; but we cannot say with any propriety that man became God. God merely assumed what is human; but this human element never existed before the assumption. If it had existed it would have had a separate personality. Now it would be against the nature of Hypostatic Union to unite Divine Personality with a pre-existing complete human being having already personal existence.'

In other words, the reason why it cannot be said that man became God is this, that the human part of Christ never had 'a personal existence of its own.' The Godhead that created it in Mary's womb performed the functions of personality in it from the first moment of its existence.

This, and no other, is the reason why the two propositions, 'God became man, and man became God,' are not convertible propositions. Divine Personality existed in Itself from eternity, before it discharged the office of personality to a human nature. But the human nature never existed before it was given Divine Personality. Its creation and its being raised to Divine Personality are not two divisible moments.

But, on the other hand, St. Thomas admits the convertibility of the two propositions: 'God is man, and man is God.' It is the '*factum est*' (' became ') the theologian does not like when Christ's human nature is spoken of in connection with the possession of perfect Divinity. Only a pre-existing thing becomes properly something new, has new relations, new functions. St. John describes in his first chapter the life of the Word before the Word ' became flesh.' There is no history of Christ's humanity before it ' became divine.' Its history starts with its being supported in existence by the Personality of the Word.

But man *is* God, and God *is* man. For some minds the first formula is more prolific in spiritual consolations; for other minds the second formula is more delightful. One is as good as the other, from the point of view of theological accuracy.

By the first we mean that Divine Personality has replaced human personality; by the second we look directly at the human element having its existence through Divine Personality. The first is no narrowing down of limitless infinitude, the second is limitless broadening of finiteness.

CHAPTER XI

A SCHOLASTIC HYPOTHESIS

It is not immensely more difficult to admit Hypostatic Union than any other supernatural grace. The moment we grant that Christ is a superman in a way in which no other human being has been or ever will be a superman, we are amongst those who can no longer have any rational difficulties against Hypostatic Union.

The Christ of the orthodox is essentially a Christ so great that He cannot be the outcome of a cosmic process, however prolonged and however potent that process may be; Christ is what He is through a direct action, or unction, to use a scriptural word, on the part of the extra-mundane Deity. That such unction should be the communication of Divine Personality itself, instead of mere finite graces, is not a new difficulty. The supernatural order once admitted, communication of Divine Personality is merely the highest possible form of supernatural elevation.

Here I should like to quote one of the side

A SCHOLASTIC HYPOTHESIS

issues of the theological doctrines on the Hypostatic Union. St. Thomas, with his masterful grip of the main question at stake, makes various suppositions, which he answers with a view to making the main point more clear. He asks whether a divine person could have taken into Hypostatic Union several individual human natures. His answer is in the affirmative; for no finite number of individual human natures could exhaust the communicability of the Divine Personality. In other words, the unction we call Hypostatic Union could have been multiplied a millionfold if God in His wisdom had chosen to do so, just as other inferior graces are multiplied.

I dare say that with many minds Hypostatic Union is a real difficulty because they shrink from the thought of the Godhead being contained and circumscribed within the limits of a created nature. To them Incarnation seems hardly possible without a loss to Divinity itself. Their instinct is right. No amount of spiritual advantage in the creature could ever be an adequate compensation for any loss to the Majesty of the Godhead itself. In fact, the idea implies contradiction. How could loss to God ever be the creature's gain, as all the creature's happiness is precisely in the creature's aspiration to an immutably happy Divinity? A diminished or humbled Godhead would be the creature's greatest misfortune.

Hypostatic Union leaves the potentialities of Godhead as infinite as it found them. 'The power of a Divine Person is infinite; it cannot be limited down to any created thing. Therefore we have to say that the Divine Person did not take unto Itself our human nature in such a wise as not to be able to take up another nature. For in such a case it would seem that the personality of a divine nature is thus included within one single human nature, that no other nature could have been united with such a Divine Personality—a thing that is absurd. 'The uncreated can never be included within the created. It is clear therefore that whether we consider the Divine Person from the point of view of its power, which is the (effective) principle of the union, or whether we consider it from the point of view of personality itself, which is the goal of the union, we have to admit that the Divine Person could have taken up a numerically distinct human nature from the one which it took in fact.' [1]

With such views on the resources of Divinity, the main objection against Hypostatic Union falls to the ground. Hypostatic Union is infinite glory and sanctity to the human nature without its being the least fettering of the freedom of Godhead itself.

St. Thomas conceives the possibility of a higher kind of Incarnation than the one which Faith

[1] Pt. iii., quest. 3, art. 7.

teaches. A Hypostatic Union in which the three divine persons take up one single individual nature. The idea implies no contradiction. 'Non est impossibile divinis personis ut duae vel tres assumant unam naturam humanam.'[1]

Even in this highest form of divine liberality we find God's free choice, which is the charm of all His gifts. Where there are many possibilities, He chooses the one best adapted for a particular purpose. Hypostatic Union is no exception to the rule of the divine deliberateness in giving. Not only is Hypostatic Union God's free election, but the kind of Hypostatic Union He determines upon shows infinitely wise thought. God is never overwhelmed by His own liberalities. In the thirteenth century, as much as in our own, there was the milk and honey temperament of the optimist. I take optimism here in its philosophical sense. I mean the man who thinks that God ought always to do the best possible thing, irrespective of the results on the purport of the whole. So the idea that a Divine Personality might have united with itself every human individual in oneness of person made them ask the question why God in His charity did not do so.

St. Thomas gives those big children satisfaction (if a born optimist can ever be satisfied) in the fifth article of the ninth question. 'If we all were united hypostatically, there would not have been

[1] Quest. 3, art. 6.

the marvel of marvels, the charity of Christ dying on the Cross for us.' Such is the meaning of one of his reasonings. It is a profound one, because it shows that the great marvel in the whole mystery of the Incarnation is not so much the initial fact of the Hypostatic Union as the human life and death of the God-man. 'I answer that the love of God towards men shows itself not only in taking up the human nature, but much more (*præcipue*) through the things He suffered in the human nature for other men, according to Rom. v. 8, "God commendeth His charity towards us, because when as yet we were sinners, Christ died for us." This could not have taken place, if He had taken up human nature in all its representatives.'[1]

The divine act or fact of the Hypostatic Union, wonderful as it is, is to the mind of the theologian not the main point. The marvel of marvels is the life of which the Hypostatic Union is the beginning.

What a glorious theology! Far from being overpowered by the doctrine of a Divine Person uniting a human nature in an indissoluble oneness, it makes the value of such exaltation subservient to the experimental sanctity of conscious life and activity.

[1] Pt. 3, quest. 5, art. 5, ad. 2.

CHAPTER XII

'INSTRUMENTUM CONJUNCTUM DIVINITATIS'

SPEAKING metaphorically, I said in a previous chapter that the spiritual vitalities in Christ's Person are like so many ramifications of a great tidal river flowing on such even land as would allow the waters of the ocean to mix with the waters of the river over the whole course of the stream.

The great aim of our theology is to make Christ's human nature as divine as possible whilst preserving the real distinction between His humanity and His Divinity. St. Thomas, by a rare stroke of genius, has found the theological formula that states this highest possible elevation of Christ's humanity by His Divinity for the active purposes of the Redemption. Christ's humanity is to His Divinity a live instrument, *instrumentum conjunctum Divinitatis*. It is one of the finest concepts of Catholic theology, and a concept too which is indispensable if the scriptures have to be taken in their literal meaning. The theory is briefly this : My arm and my hand are the live or the joined instruments of my brain.

Being vitally connected with my brain, there is practically no limit to the perfection of rational work my hand, with no gift of reason residing in it, may achieve. The hand of Michael Angelo has painted the Last Judgment and created the wonderful Moses; it was his hand that did it, but not his hand alone, for from his brain there streamed into his hand the creative power of genius. In scholastic language Michael Angelo's hand would be the *instrumentum conjunctum* of his brain.

Such is the view St. Thomas takes of Christ's manhood. Because Godhead is united with manhood in one Person as brain and hand are united in one organism, manhood is the hand of Godhead, manhood does the works of God just as the human hand does the works of human genius.

It is easy to see that St. Thomas has practically introduced a *tertium quid* between Godhead and manhood in Christ, something that is lower than Hypostatic Union and at the same time is higher than human nature, even in its loftiest state of sanctification. The technical name for this *tertium quid* is Divine Instrumentality. Highest in Christ there is Hypostatic Union; lowest, there is immensity of sanctifying grace; between the two there is Divine Instrumentality. It may be a matter of regret that we have no expression for it that reminds one less of mechanical things. St. Thomas has always been satisfied with the word

'INSTRUMENTUM CONJUNCTUM'

instrumentum, and it is the reader's duty to attach to this term such meaning as will make it for him the expression of highest spiritual reality.

I shall state now this great doctrine in the words of St. Thomas himself; in their conciseness they open out wonderful horizons of spiritual possibilities, of which we the redeemed are naturally the beneficiaries. I quote from the second article of the thirteenth question of the third part of the Summa. 'The soul of Christ may be viewed under a double aspect. There is first the soul's congenital nature, with its power either natural or gratuitous (i.e. supernatural); then we may view the soul of Christ as the instrument of the Word of God hypostatically united with it. Speaking then of the soul of Christ from the point of view of its congenital nature and power either supernatural or gratuitous, the soul of Christ has in itself the power of bringing about those effects which are natural to the soul, as, for instance, to rule over the body and to dispose the human acts, and also to enlighten through the fulness of its grace and knowledge all those rational creatures who fall short of the perfection which is in Christ's soul, in the way in which it is possible for a reasoning creature to be thus illuminated.

'But if now we speak of Christ's soul from the point of view of its being the instrument of the Word united with it (hypostatically), from **that** point of view Christ's soul had the instrumental power to bring about all those miraculous changes which in any way have any relation to the end of the Incarnation, which is to restore all things either in the heavens or on the earth. But such changes in creatures as would bring about their annihilation are the counterpart of the creation of things out of nothing, and therefore as God alone is able to create out of nothing, God alone has power to annihilate creatures, for God alone keeps beings in their existence lest they fall back into nothingness. Therefore we must say that the soul of Christ is not possessed with Omnipotence concerning the mutation of created things.'

We see therefore that there is only one exception to the extent of Christ's power as the live instrument of the Word: creation out of nothing and the corresponding power of annihilation could not be attributed to our Lord as man; short of that, there is nothing which Our Lord could not do. The resurrection of the bodies at the end of the world is perhaps the highest external manifestation of Our Lord's power; it is within Our Lord's power to bring back to life every human organism, because the resurrection of all flesh is not creation out of nothing, but reconstruction out of previous materials. ' For as the Father raiseth up the dead and giveth life, so the Son also giveth life to whom He will, for neither does the Father judge any man, but

'INSTRUMENTUM CONJUNCTUM'

has given all judgement to the Son, that all men may honour the Son as they honour the Father . . . Amen, Amen, I say unto you, that the hour cometh and now is when the dead shall hear the voice of the Son of God, and they that hear shall live, for as the Father has life in Himself, so He has given to the Son also to have life in Himself. . . . I cannot of myself do anything. As I hear, so I judge, and My judgment is just : because I seek not My own will, but the will of Him that sent me.'[1]

'Now this is the Will of the Father who sent Me, that of all that He has given Me I should lose nothing, but should raise it up again in the last day; and this is the Will of My Father that sent Me, that everyone who seeth the Son and believeth in Him may have life everlasting, and I will raise him up in the last day. . . . He that eateth My Flesh and drinketh My Blood has everlasting life, and I will raise him up in the last day.'[2]

'Our conversation is in heaven, from whence also we look for the Saviour, Our Lord Jesus Christ, who will reform the body of our lowness, made like to the body of His glory, according to the operation whereby also He is able to subdue all things unto Himself.'[3]

'Afterwards the end, when He [i.e. Christ] shall have delivered up the Kingdom to God and the Father, when He shall have brought to nought all

[1] St. John v.   [2] St. John vi.   [3] Phil. iii. 20, 21.

principality and power and virtue; for He must reign until He has put all enemies under His feet, and the enemy Death shall be destroyed last; for He hath put all things under His feet; whereas he says all things are put under Him, undoubtedly He is excepted who put all things under Him, and when all things shall be subdued unto Him, then the Son also Himself shall be subject unto Him that put all things under Him, that God may be all in all.'[1]

Texts like the foregoing—and it would be easy to quote many more to the same effect—point clearly to a power in Our Lord's Personality which is not the power of the Godhead itself, but is a power of Christ's manhood and yet it is a power which is almost omnipotent. Scholastic theologians have expressed it in a formula of their own coining: 'The instrumental power of Christ'—'*Instrumentum Verbi Dei.*' It expresses the most wonderful thing in the simplest terms.

As I have already insinuated, from this central principle there flow many spiritual possibilities; and here I want the reader to pay great attention to another doctrine of St. Thomas which is merely a corollary of the doctrine already enunciated. Our Lord's life, death, resurrection, and ascension are the instruments of Divinity for our sanctification, our life, our resurrection, and our ascension. It is clear, of course, that Our Lord is our model, in

[1] 1 Cor. xv. 24-28.

His life, death, resurrection, and ascension. It is clear again that Our Lord through His life and death atoned for us, merited for us, prayed for us; such causal influences on the part of Our Lord with respect to mankind are called moral influences, moral causes. But there is more, and there must be more, if scriptural expressions as well as the language of Catholic tradition are not to be treated as hyperbolical. Christ's death is our life; Christ's resurrection is our resurrection.

There is nothing more instructive from this point of view than to read the whole of the forty-eighth question of the third part of the Summa: 'On the way in which Our Lord's passion brought about our salvation.' First article: ' Did Christ's passion cause our salvation by manner of merit ? ' The answer is of course in the affirmative. Second article: ' Did Christ's passion cause our salvation by manner of satisfaction ? ' Again the answer is in the affirmative. Third article: ' Did Christ's passion cause our salvation by manner of a sacrifice?' Again he says Yes. Fourth and fifth articles: ' Did Christ, and Christ alone, cause our salvation by manner of redemption ? ' The answer is affirmative to both parts of the question. Sixth and last article: ' Did Christ's passion cause our salvation by manner of efficiency ? ' (*per modum efficientiae*). Efficiency in scholastic language is physical efficiency as opposed to a moral claim.

'My answer is this,' says St. Thomas; 'there is a double set of efficient agents, the principal agent and the instrumental agent: the principal efficient agent of the human salvation is God. But as Christ's humanity is the instrument of Divinity, as said already, through a direct consequence all the actions and sufferings of Christ work out instrumentally under the power of Divinity the human salvation, and therefore Christ's passion causes human salvation by way of efficiency.'

In this same article St. Thomas quotes an objection to this great theory. The objection is this: There is no effective bodily action except through contact; but Christ's passion could not have contact with all men; therefore He could not bring about the salvation of all men by means of a physical efficiency. I quote the answer literally:—

'To the second objection I reply that though the passion of Christ be a bodily phenomenon, it has spiritual power from the Divinity that is united with it, and therefore it has efficiency by means of a spiritual contact—that is to say, by faith, and the sacrament of faith.'

This last clause, 'by faith, and the sacrament of faith,' means this: that faith in individual souls by which they are saved is caused by Christ's passion, in the manner of an efficiency. To receive faith is to be touched by Christ's passion. With greater clearness still is this doctrine stated in the sixth article of the fiftieth question. There St. Thomas asks whether Christ's death did anything for our salvation. By death he means, not exactly the act of dying, but the actual state of death. There is an obvious objection : the dead Christ could not merit, from the very fact of His being dead ; therefore though the dying Christ might merit, the dead Christ could not do anything for us. ' Yes,' says St. Thomas, ' the dead Christ could not be the cause of our salvation, in the manner of merit, but he could be a cause of salvation in the manner of an efficiency, because even in death Divinity was not separated from Our Lord's Flesh, and therefore whatever happened to Our Lord's dead Body is to us a source of salvation in virtue of the Divinity united with it.'

The same doctrine occurs again with the causality of Our Lord's resurrection. I cannot resist the temptation of quoting once more ; my quotation is taken from the first article of the fifty-sixth question. ' Christ's resurrection,' says St. Thomas, ' is the efficient cause of our resurrection because Christ's Humanity precisely from being a risen humanity is in a way the instrument of His Divinity, and works in the power of the Divinity, and therefore as all other things which Christ did in his Humanity or suffered in His Humanity are to us a source of salvation in virtue of His Divinity, Christ's resurrection also is an efficient cause of our resurrection through Divine Power, to whom it belongs to quicken the dead; for this Divine Power is present to and has contact with all places and all times; and this contact of power suffices to explain that efficiency of Christ's resurrection.'

In an earlier question of this third part of the Summa [1] St. Thomas has another application of this great principle. Through it he explains the possibility for Christ to be the life-giving Head to the heavenly spirits in His Humanity. How could humanity be to angelic spirits the source of spiritual perfection? 'Christ's Humanity,' says St. Thomas, 'in virtue of the spiritual nature, that is the Divine nature, is able to cause something (spiritual) not only in the spirits of men, but also in the spirits of angels, on account of that most intimate union of the Humanity with God—that is to say, Hypostatic Union.' Christ gives something spiritual to the angels through His Humanity, but the Humanity does it in virtue of the Divinity. It is again the Divine Instrumentality.

I do not think I owe the reader an apology for keeping him so long in these high theological regions; the Church's greatest divine, St. Thomas, can never be understood unless we grasp his principles of the Divine Instrumentality in connection

[1] Quest. 8, art. 4.

with our Lord's Humanity. If once we grasp it, it becomes a most sweet, a most devotional principle. We shall feel soon how near we are, after all, in our spiritual life to Christ's life, death, and resurrection. Nothing will surprise us any more in what we read of the mystical unions of the life of the saint with Christ's life. Infinite, unchanging, all-present Divinity, for whom there is no yesterday nor to-morrow, simply uses the actions of Our Lord as a most beautiful tool for the sanctification of souls. Christ's death on the Cross is as truly and as directly the cause of my sanctification in the hands of Godhead as the pen with which I write is the cause of the letters that cover the paper on which I write. The mystical possibilities of this great theory of St. Thomas are greater than anything we could imagine.

In one of the above quotations from St. Thomas the great doctor says that Christ's Humanity, precisely because it is a risen humanity, is a fit instrument in the hands of God to bring about our own resurrection. We must remember what we said at the beginning, that every instrument has a fitness of its own for a definite and specific purpose. Christ is the fit instrument of our resurrection because He is a *risen* Christ. We may say likewise that Our Lord is a fit instrument of every kind of sanctification and spiritual purification because

He has suffered in His Body, because at one time His Body was a dead body; through His passion and death His Humanity acquired a most eminent fitness to be in the hands of God the instrument of the most miraculous graces and resurrections.

From all that precedes we see how the whole supernatural world rests on the shoulders of Christ's Humanity. In the whole work of our salvation and sanctification Christ's Divinity does not come in, except as the higher cause. We know that Divinity is behind it all, yet Divinity, being infinite truth and reality, never allows the Humanity to shirk any work that may possibly be done by Humanity. There is only one instance in which Divinity as such is directly appealed to in the work of our salvation: it is the adequate reparation given to God's offended majesty. Of this I shall say more later on. In everything else it is the Humanity that does the work. It does it indeed as the instrument of Divinity, but it does it none the less directly.

To come back to our original comparison, we may navigate for a long time on the stream of Christ's human life and Christ's human perfection; we may do marvels like those that go down to the sea, we may see great wonders long before we have to come to the ocean of His Divinity.

The thought of this omnipotence of Our Lord's Humanity ought to be to us a source of peace and rest. 'These things I have spoken to you that in Me you may have peace; in the world you shall have distress; but have confidence, I have overcome the world.'[1]

In Our Lord Himself we see the grandest realisation of a deep spiritual principle enunciated by Him in the Gospel of St. Luke. 'He that has shall receive and he shall abound, and he that has not, even what he has shall be taken away from him.'

Hypostatic Union, far from making Our Lord's Humanity complete, requires in our Lord's Humanity the presence of a new gift: the gift of sanctifying grace.

Sanctifying grace is not Divinity itself, it is something created; it is the greatest possible resemblance with God which a spirit may possess. Sanctifying grace differs entirely from the Divine Instrumentality spoken of above. Yet it is owing to the fact of the Hypostatic Union and to the fact of the Divine Instrumentality that sanctifying grace is in Our Lord.

Sanctifying grace is a necessary concomitant in Christ's soul of Hypostatic Union and Divine Instrumentality. St. Thomas devotes the seventh and eighth questions of the third part to Our Lord's sanctifying grace. In the first article of the seventh question he says that the reasons why there must be in Our Lord sanctifying grace are precisely

[1] St. John xvi. 33.

Hypostatic Union and Divine Instrumentality. Christ's soul is united with Divinity, but Christ's soul is not Divinity itself. To be united with Divinity does not make it into Divinity, therefore it must be made as divine as possible, it must resemble Divinity as closely as possible ; this is done through sanctifying grace. Union between two is thinkable only when the two remain two distinct beings in the union ; if they became one being it would be no longer a union, but a fusion ; therefore in Hypostatic Union Our Lord's humanity remains quite distinct. This is why the presence of Divinity, far from rendering sanctifying grace superfluous, makes its possession of much greater necessity for Our Lord than for any other creature, otherwise the union would be an ill-assorted union.

Then again, from the point of view of Divine Instrumentality, sanctifying grace becomes an absolute necessity for Our Lord. ' Christ's Humanity,' says St. Thomas, ' is the instrument of Divinity, but He is not like an inanimate instrument, which has no action of its own, but is merely moved by a higher agent ; He is, on the contrary, an instrument that is animated by a rational soul, which in the very act of being used has an action of its own, and therefore for the sake of congenital action He was bound to have sanctifying grace.'

[1] Quest. 7, art. 1.

'INSTRUMENTUM CONJUNCTUM'

The whole Humanity of Christ must be thought of as being first permeated with spiritual vitalities, such as sanctifying grace, before it could be a fit instrument for man's sanctification in the hands of God; without those spiritual vitalities the instrument would have lacked natural fitness.

To what extent did our Lord possess sanctifying grace? Fulness of grace is constantly attributed to our Lord. St. Thomas says it was not actually infinite grace; but it was such a grace as to establish a kind of proportion between Christ's soul and Christ's Divinity. He has as much grace as is necessary to make the union between the human soul and Divinity a well-assorted union. God alone therefore could measure the extent of Our Lord's grace. God alone could be judge of the measure of sanctifying grace that would make of Christ's Humanity a fit and harmonious instrument in the hands of Divinity.

It would be a dangerous tendency if the keen realisation of our spiritual privileges and responsibilities were to make us overlook Our Lord's Humanity for the sake of something exclusively spiritual. Catholic doctrine never detaches man's attention from Our Lord's Humanity. Christ's action as man is the greatest spirit-reality for the redeemed soul. Where spiritual life is highest and sincerest, devotion to Our Lord's Humanity is tenderest and the feeling of dependence on Him strongest. It may be stated as an unquestionable principle that Our Lord in His manhood is to the human spirit everything that makes it great and happy.

We know little of Our Lord's relation with the angels, except that He is the head and king of angels; but to the human spirit in the present life and in the future He is much more.

The expressions of the inspired scriptures, where are stated Our Lord's relations to man, and more particularly to the soul of man, are astoundingly energetic. Christ is made unto us wisdom, and justice, and sanctification, and redemption. He is our life, He is our resurrection; as in Adam we all fell, so in Christ we shall all rise; and there are a hundred other expressions that all point to much more direct and real influence of Our Lord on every soul than we commonly suppose.

CHAPTER XIII

THE AIM OF HYPOSTATIC UNION

THE presence of the Second Person of the Godhead in the individual human nature is essentially, though not exclusively, dynamic ; it is essentially a power that elevates the assumed individual human nature.

It is perhaps a theological view of which it may be said that it has become slightly obscured even amongst Catholic theologians of the latter days ; but there is no doubt as to the position which this view holds in the Christology of St. Thomas Aquinas. It is a very refreshing view, and one that may be called most appropriately, as I said, the dynamic view of Hypostatic Union.

In more recent theological works the view taken of the presence of the Divinity in the individual human nature is exclusively what I might call the static view. Theologians accept the fact of the Hypostatic Union, of the presence of the fulness of Godhead in Christ's Humanity, and there they remain. From such presence they all conclude the infinite moral dignity of Christ. A human nature that bears within itself the fulness of Godhead, that is united hypostatically with the Second Person of the Trinity, shares in the infinitude of sanctity and dignity proper to Godhead itself. They say, for instance, that Christ's sufferings had infinite atoning power because they were the sufferings of a human organism hypostatically united to Godhead. But beyond that communication of infinitude of moral worth, the more recent theologies know little of an influence of the Divine Person on the human nature in Christ; their view of the Hypostatic Union, as I said, is exclusively a static view.

The two terms 'static' and 'dynamic' are not contradictory; the same thing may be partly static, partly dynamic; so I should say that the view of St. Thomas is a combination of the static and the dynamic. For him Hypostatic Union is indeed the presence of the Divinity in an individual human nature, but it is a presence full of activities, full of vital influences; it is more than a mere communication of moral worth; it is an elevation of all the vital powers of Christ's Humanity, natural and supernatural.

This is merely another view, another statement, of his beloved expression that Christ's Humanity is in all things *instrumentum conjunctum Divinitatis*. Divinity, through Hypostatic Union, through that intimacy of presence implied in Hypostatic Union,

THE AIM OF HYPOSTATIC UNION   87

has become the master of that Humanity in a way that is not possible outside Hypostatic Union, and, owing to that complete and wonderful mastery, God does in Christ works of the spiritual order, which it would not be possible for any created nature to be the agent of, unless that nature were hypostatically united with Divinity.

More simply I should state the matter thus: Hypostatic Union is not a thing that exists for its own sake, but it is the necessary means to raise up an individual human nature to such a height as to make it capable of doing the work of human redemption and sanctification. In Hypostatic Union God has shown forth His power, because He has raised up a human nature to such a height as to make it capable of the whole work of redemption and sanctification. Christ's human soul and human body, through being united hypostatically with the Second Person of the Trinity, has acquired unparalleled fitness to be in the hands of God the instrument of every spiritual marvel—a fitness which a human nature could never possess outside Hypostatic Union. No amount of sanctifying grace could give such fitness, and it may be said that this fitness is precisely the whole aim of Hypostatic Union.

It is easy to see how the older view, which I call in modern phraseology the dynamic view of Hypostatic Union, considerably affects Christian piety.

The human being we love under the name of Jesus is the main object in the whole of our Christology. It is that human being that atones for our sins; it is that human being that directly forgives our sins; it is that human being that directly raises from their corruption those that are spiritually and physically dead; it is that human being that directly is the Father of the whole spiritual world to come. How can a man do these things? is the old objection. No man can do it, is the answer, unless he be hypostatically united with God; but being once hypostatically united with Divinity, man has a native fitness to do all those things. He does them in virtue of His Divinity, it is true; but it would be wrong to think that by this expression, ' in virtue of His Divinity,' is meant an exclusively divine action, in the sense that the God who dwells in Christ does it. No, it is that human being called Jesus who does it, and He has become capable of doing it simply because He is hypostatically united with Godhead; without such union He could never do such works.

The merely static view of the presence of Divinity in Christ through Hypostatic Union might easily lead to a concept of Christ's Personality that accentuates the duality of natures in Him at the expense of the union of the two natures. With all due reverence, might I be allowed to say that there is a danger of our thinking of Christ in layers, with the consequent feeling of unreality?

THE AIM OF HYPOSTATIC UNION

The older theology was as firm a believer in the differences of the two natures in Christ, the divine and the human; but the two natures for the older theology are not two separate layers of life in Christ's Personality; there is a most intimate compenetration of activities between the two natures, the divine nature using the human nature as its *instrumentum conjunctum,* as my brain uses my arm and my hand, according to the favourite simile of St. Thomas.

The identification of the two natures and their confusion into one entity is the old Eutychian heresy, the most subtle aberration of man trying to understand the psychology of Christ. St. Thomas has shown how it is possible to conceive a compenetration of the two natures that is not a confusion—the compenetration of mutual activities.

The Son of Man stands before us in the fulness of Divine Power; and Divinity, far from diminishing His manhood, has given that Humanity undreamed of powers and possibilities that will make every human heart in this world and in the next find shelter in Him as the birds of the air find shelter in the mighty tree that springs up from the mustard seed.

CHAPTER XIV

THE TWO WILLS AND THE TWO OPERATIONS IN CHRIST

A STUDY of the theological controversies of the early church-periods reveals a different temper from the temper of the controversies of a later date. Christians were evidently deeply interested in Christ's Personality and in Christ's psychology—I might almost say in Christ's intimate life. Perhaps it is more congenial to the Eastern mind to analyse its God than to analyse itself. Western doctrinal upheavals have always been more or less about practical things, about good works, about sanctity, about sacraments. We are indebted, however, to the East and its theologians for that most perfect Christology which is the Church's greatest treasure.

Controversies about the two wills and the two operations in Christ were the last stages of the great theological battle; the sixth and seventh centuries are full of them, both ecclesiastically and politically. Monothelitism is the received name for the wrong standpoint in that matter;

TWO WILLS AND TWO OPERATIONS 91

it means oneness of will, whilst the Church decided for a duality of wills and a duality of operations in Christ.

The Council of Ephesus had defined the oneness of person in Christ; the Council of Chalcedon had defined the duality of natures in Christ. Christ has a divine nature and a human nature in one personality. That new doubts should have sprung up is comprehensible enough; Christ's will was always one with His Father's will, Christ's actions were always in obedience to His Father's commands; so it would seem that, in spite of the duality of nature, there was oneness of will and oneness of operation. The error was a subtle one, and no doubt the holiest men might be deceived. After all, oneness with God's will is highest sanctity. The Latin Church, whose theology prevailed in the long run, considered that oneness of will and oneness of operation would be a partial renewing of the older heresy of Eutyches. Will and operation are nature's best jewels; if they are one only in Christ and not two, duality of nature is of little avail; so there is in Christ the divine will and the human will, the divine operation and the human operation.

This much for the historical and dogmatic stating of the question. But duality of will and operation in Christ is a point of theology full of interest to those to whom the Christ-psychology is the most entrancing psychology. The Eastern mind that fell into Monothelitism overlooked a distinction which many other minds have overlooked : the distinction between the will as a power and the will as an object. There can never be identification of powers, but there may be identification of objects. When I say that my will and somebody's will are one, I mean to say that we strive after the same object, that we love the same object, that we agree about the same object ; so in Christ there never was, and there never could be, two wills—in the sense of two conflicting and contradictory objects ; whatever was willed by Divinity was also willed by humanity. Such an identification of will is a perfection ; fusion of wills as powers would be, on the contrary, a great loss ; it would be, in fact, the destruction of nature.

But there is one consideration which is of utmost importance both in Christ's psychology and in our own psychology : how far is that oneness of object preserved in the reluctance of our will powers when we have to do a hard thing which we know to be God's will, or, more clearly, the object of God's will. That there was such a reluctance in Christ is evident from His prayer and agony in the garden, related more explicitly by St. Luke and alluded to by St. Matthew and St. Mark. ' My soul is sorrowful even unto death.' [1]

[1] St. Mark xiv. 34.

That there was a tremendous struggle in Christ's soul at that hour is evident from the sweat of blood. Yet oneness of will with the Father's will was part of Christ's unalterable sanctity. The solution of this apparent contradiction lies in the distinction between the higher human will and the lower human will. The higher will is made of reason, the lower will is made of sensations and impressions. The two wills may follow different lines—opposite lines even; it is man's struggle, which is not always a struggle between good and evil, but is as frequently a struggle between the higher good and the lower good. Now oneness with the divine will is preserved through the stability of the higher will, that it should carry out its purpose even against the most stubborn reluctance of the will of impression. Such was Christ's oneness of will. 'Abba, Father, all things are possible to Thee; remove this chalice from me: but not what I will, but what Thou wilt.'[1] That duality of will which the Catholic Church adopted as part of her Christology is really the most beautiful trait in our theology of Christ, because in it we find the glorification of human freedom wonderfully combined with the oneness of the divine purpose.

St. Thomas Aquinas, who is as great a believer in the duality of wills and operations in Christ as

[1] St. Mark xiv. 36.

any other theologian, has conceived another oneness of will besides the oneness of objects. I quote him literally from the first article of the nineteenth question, in the answer to the second objection. 'Therefore the operation which is of the human nature in Christ, as far as it is the instrument of Divinity, is not different from the operation of the Divinity; for the salvation through which Christ's humanity saves is not different from the salvation through which His Divinity saves.'

In this sentence we have practically all that oneness in Christ's life we want ; it is a deep concept to say that there are not two savings in Christ, one done by His Divinity and one done by His humanity ; on the contrary, it is all one act, owing to the wonderful instrumental elevation and influence, made so much of by St. Thomas.

No doubt, thoughts of that kind had been floating in the Eastern mind. Salvation was God's work, God's will, God's love ; it could not think of a dual salvation. But it was reserved to a Western genius to show how with a duality of wills and powers there could be oneness of operation.

CHAPTER XV

CHRIST'S KNOWLEDGE

OUR theology on Christ's knowledge is guided completely by a twofold entirety in Christ—namely, He is entirely human, and He is a principle of life to the entirety of the human race.

The various classes of knowledge which theology attributes to our Lord are as indispensable to this twofold function of His as our nerves and sinews are indispensable to us in order to make of our body a healthy, active, agile body, whose very life is a feeling of refreshing well-being.

At first sight the conclusions of theology in this matter may seem arbitrary; it might appear as if the theologian had fallen into the trap that lies before every theological idealistic hero-worshipper and millennium dreamer: you simply make your hero stand for every beautiful abstraction; once in the dreamland of sanctity, there is no more reason to draw the line than there is in fairyland. A mountain of gold is as easily imagined as a house of gold. As Christ is the ideal, and must be the ideal, we simply hang on Him all the spiritual glories we can think of, and afterwards we call it theology. Such, I say, might be the cautious attitude even of a reverential mind towards a theologian's wisdom. Is it anything else, says the critical reader, than an ordinary instance of that love of accumulation so noticeable in the hero-worshipper?

Careful study of the argumentation of the masters of sacred wisdom in that matter reveals a quite different temper : it is not the temper of the idealist, it is the temper of the psychologist. The theology of our Lord's knowledge is analytic, not synthetic ; if it postulates various classes of knowledge in our Lord, it postulates them as life-functions, not as the ornaments of an infinitely privileged nature. Theology simply says that without those various kinds of knowledge Christ could never be entirely human, that He could never be the life of the entire human race.

So little indeed has the naïve love of the hero-worshipper for the accumulation of glories given the tune in this matter, that this point has, on the contrary, acquired a kind of secondary celebrity in the history of theology for a retractation of St. Thomas based on psychological considerations. In his earlier works St. Thomas had held the opinion that in Christ there was no kind of acquired knowledge of the experimental class. This view he retracts as being contrary to a deeper understanding of the workings of Christ's human nature.

CHRIST'S KNOWLEDGE

Before proceeding, I must give the reader a synoptic view of the various kinds of rational knowledge of which Catholic theology speaks. The classification is short, including only four members. But it is a classification which is absolutely indispensable to theology; without it many of the revealed truths would lack rational meaning.

First and highest is the divine knowledge, the knowledge which God has of Himself and of everything else besides. This is increated knowledge.

Then, coming to the rational creature, there is the Blessed Vision of God, called technically 'beatific vision.' It is an entirely supernatural, I might almost say an entirely miraculous, kind of knowledge, granted only to the spirits perfect in charity and having reached the goal of eternal fixity in goodness. By means of this knowledge a spirit, either human or angelic, is enabled to see God in His own native splendour, and he is enabled to see in God many things of which God is the origin, and of which God has knowledge.

After that we come to spirit-knowledge properly so-called. A pure spirit is created with the full knowledge of all things that are equal to him, or lower than himself, besides his having a partial knowledge of beings higher than himself. This knowledge does not depend, in its essentials, on sanctity; even a fallen spirit retains it. Such knowledge is complete in the spirit's mind from the first moment of his existence. No new ideas come to the spirit, except by special grace. But there may be new applications of the innate idea. The spirit's perfection is such as to postulate that initial fulness of wisdom.

The fourth kind of rational knowledge belongs to the human spirit, in its state of union with the body. It is the knowledge acquired by the mind through the infinitely varied instrumentality of the senses. It is the wonderful schooling through the external world, with its ever new experiences and surprises, not to speak of its great lessons and possible discoveries.

I need not enter into all the divisions and varieties that may be found within each of the four categories. I mention, as it were, four continents, four planes of intellectual activities; but I lay no claim to having said anything as to the manifold wonders that may be hidden within their boundaries.

Leaving alone the first kind of knowledge mentioned, God's knowledge in Himself and of Himself, and which is a divine and unchanging act, the three other kinds of knowledge, created knowledge, may vary endlessly in extent and vividness according to the sanctity or perfection of the individual, human or angelic. Moreover—and this is a point of utmost importance in theological matters—the three kinds may be in the same mind, at the same time, regarding the same objects of knowledge. In other words, there is no apparent contradiction in the assumption that a human being may know all about another human being, at the same time, in the vision of God, in the angelic mode of knowledge, and in virtue of sense observation. Each mode of knowing would convey something which the other modes fail to convey, and the more perfect mode would not render useless the services of the less perfect mode, because the less perfect mode represents many times its object in a more congenital and more proportionate way.

Daily experiences supply easy analogies. I may know of some clever piece of mechanical skill from a friend's description or from reading; both the book and the friend give me a very good idea of the invention. After that I may go to the town where it is on view and look at it myself. Though I walk up to it with a very good image of it in my brain, when I actually come to see it, my store of experiences is the richer for the sight. I may then begin a process of mental investigation; I try to fathom the principle of the invention; I may succeed in following in my own mind the road which the original inventor followed in his, and I may be led to the same conclusions, and arrive concerning that very thing at the knowledge which its maker had before he carried his thoughts into execution. Here we have three different modes of knowing the same object; far from excluding or superseding each other, they help each other towards a fuller comprehension of the little wonder. This is of course a mere analogy to illustrate a much higher train of thought: how, for instance, there may be new intellectual gratification to meet the thing that was seen in the light of God's vision, as a reflection in a mirror, outside God, in its own native individuality, through another and lower mode of knowledge.

In Christ there are at the same time all the aforesaid kinds of knowledge : there is the infinite, the divine knowledge of the Godhead; there is the threefold created knowledge of beatific vision, of angelic cognition, and of human experience and ratiocination.

In our thoughts on the Incarnation there is the constant danger of being overwhelmed by the fact of Christ's Divinity, as if it were the all-absorbing and all-effacing splendour of Christ's wonderful Personality. But we ought to bear in mind the great truth that Divinity was united with humanity not so much for the sake of that union, however adorable it may be, as for the sake of the great human life such a union rendered possible. So in this matter of knowledge, the presence of the divine mind in Christ's person, far from rendering superfluous the glories of the human mind, has no other end in view than precisely the perfection of that human mind. This is why St. Thomas says that if in Christ's Person there had been divine knowledge only, Christ's soul would have been in the dark, and its being united with the Godhead would have been a useless privilege. Hypostatic Union took place in order to cause in Christ's human soul such bliss, such lights, as to make of it in its turn the direct source and cause of all the bliss and all the light that will flood the minds of the elect, in the clear vision of God, for all eternity. It would not seem as if such a height and such a power of beatific vision as to make it the efficient cause of all other beatific visions, in ordinary human minds, were at all possible unless Divine Personality, which is the Wisdom of God the Father, were united with that created mind. Unless Christ had been endowed with beatific vision He could not have been happy in Himself; He could not have become to us the efficient cause of our own vision of God; He could not have possessed that double entirety of glorified humanity that makes Him what He is.

This same principle of Christ's entirety makes it imperative on the theologian to ascribe to Him a most complete and a most far-reaching intellectual knowledge, which cannot have its origin in the experiences of sense, and which at the same time is not beatific vision. Christ's human mind must have been fully developed, must have possessed every kind of perfection a created intellect may possess, independently, so to speak, of the gift of God's vision, simply because it is the intellect of a man who has the double privilege of being God-man in Himself, and the King of the human race for ever, and, by a kind of extension, the King of the whole spirit-race. The whole created intellectual world is at His feet, because in Him the human intellect has acquired unparalleled perfection through the proximity of the Godhead.

It was precisely this incontrovertible fulness of intellectuality that made it seem doubtful whether there was any room for the workings of the ordinary human mind in Christ. Why should one so full of direct intellectual perceptions learn from the store-house of sense observations? St. Thomas himself was impressed by such considerations, as I have said already. But St. Thomas learned what we all learn when Christ is the habitual subject of our thoughts: the necessity of keeping Him as human as possible, in spite of the sublimities of the Hypostatic Union, and even, perhaps, on account of those very sublimities.

That Christ's human intellect should be filled with pure spirit-knowledge of all things belongs to the entirety of His representative rôle, embodying in Himself the whole human nature. But He would not have been in Himself an entirely human being if

He had not acted and learned precisely like a human being. Christ's human brain is the most powerful, the most active that ever was. The attribute of genius belongs to Christ more than to any other historical personage. He may be called the greatest thinker, the greatest philosopher, without any impropriety of language. He possesses in the most eminent degree what makes the really great amongst men so powerful—a serene, wonderfully penetrating mind at the service of a will of infinite resolve and considerateness. The higher kind of knowledge only comes in as a kind of reserve when the organic brain of Christ—for such is the expression best suited to render the theology of St. Thomas in this matter—has done all it could do in virtue of its own superhuman excellency. How far a created human brain under the elevating influence of Hypostatic Union can go in its potentialities is of course a matter for admiring reverence rather than for dogmatic diagnosis. St. Thomas in the first article of the twelfth question simply says that Christ knew through the sheer penetration of His human brain-power all that can be known through human induction and deduction. Such are not his words; but such is his meaning. In Christ the human mind attains its ideal perfection and power. The process of deduction and induction in Christ's mind was a progressive process, not an instantaneous one, as Christ's brain reached its maturity not instantaneously but progressively. He learned as He grew up. 'And Jesus advanced in wisdom and age, and grace with God and man.'[1]

It is a principle admitted universally that Christ, through the combined clarities of the three sorts of created knowledge here described, knows everything that concerns the human race. The whole of mankind's nature with its life and free will is reflected in Christ's mind as in a mirror. St. Thomas thinks that such knowledge constitutes actually an infinity of knowledge, as the free acts of the human individuals go on for all eternity. Such special and determined kind of infinitude is not above the grasp of a finite intellect, as it is infinitude in one direction only, not infinitude all round. What Catholic theology is at pains to show is that complete mastery of mankind by the Son of man through which our race is deified.

The theology on Christ's knowledge has received a strange actuality in our own days from unexpected quarters. Protestant theologians are at a loss how to explain Christ's abasement. This most vexed question is called the Kenotic question : How did Christ 'empty' Himself? More than one Anglican theologian explains Kenosis through deficiency in knowledge. Christ is supposed to have been lacking in knowledge in order to humble Himself, or anyhow to have turned away from

[1] St. Luke ii. 52.

knowledge—to have shut His eyes for a time to the things which He knew.

Catholic theology is as great a believer in Christ's abasement as any other theology, but it never felt the need of curtailing Christ's spiritual and intellectual privileges in order to make of Him 'a high Priest who can have compassion on our infirmities.' Fulness of knowledge, on the contrary, makes of Christ the High Priest. To make of the absence of knowledge a means of sanctity is a theological trick peculiarly distasteful to the Catholic mind; above all, one cannot see how the Son of God made man could have gained anything by willingly ignoring the facts of His Divine Sonship. Even if it had been possible for Him to exclude such knowledge from His mind, it would have been loss, not gain, to His cause, as His life must necessarily have been lowered through this very forgetfulness of His divine origin. It is a very strange phase of thought in our own days to look for moral progress to ignorance instead of to knowledge, as does the older theology.

There is only one way in which Catholic theology admits a kind of voluntary limitation of His knowledge by Christ. Catholic theology distinguishes between actual and habitual knowledge. I may know a thing and yet not consider it actually; I may even make an effort of will and turn away my mind from the actual consideration of an object, and in this sense it may even be profitable to sanctity 'to ignore.' Thus if I am asked to perform an act of kindness which is difficult to me, there might be human considerations of an inferior order of such a nature as to reconcile me with the performance of my duty. Such considerations I discard; I turn away my eyes from them; I fix my mind on higher motives, less alluring and less potent, but infinitely purer. In this case my spirituality has gained through a restriction of actual knowledge.

In Christ there was likewise actual knowledge and habitual knowledge, at least in the inferior planes of His science; but Catholic theology is most constant in asserting that Christ realised His Divinity constantly, unceasingly, with His whole being; but it is not against Catholic theology to say that Christ in the lower sphere of His knowing powers did not always consider actually all the things He knew. We are even permitted to think that Christ in His great struggle with sin, of set purpose, turned His human attention away, at times at least, from the glorious vision of the results of His cross in the world of souls, in order that He might drink the cup of bitterness with more heroic constancy. In this sense we may grant that Kenosis has something to do with knowledge. It is not exactly ignorance, but rather an absence of consideration. It is perhaps that very thing which Anglican divines are striving after when they attempt to make of ignorance in the Son of God an occasion of greater heroism. We may grant to them that our Lord at various periods, of set purpose, turned away His human attention from considerations that would have filled Him with gladness if He had allowed them to force themselves on His mind.

CHAPTER XVI

IN CHRIST

THE phrase 'in Christ' occurs nearly eighty times in St. Paul's epistles; frequently it is translated into 'by,' 'through,' 'for the sake of' Christ. Yet such alterations ought not to deprive us of the wealth of mystical meaning contained in the original phrase 'in Christ.' We have a right to the literal application of the Pauline expression. To alter it into anything less emphatic is to tamper with our spiritual inheritance.

Let us first dwell on the deep originality of the phrase, on its strangeness, if we compare it with ordinary human speech. No doubt it is this very strangeness that may have led the translators to the adoption of less significant prepositions to take the place of the 'in.'

One could hardly think of a phrase, say in English, or German, or French, or Italian, or Latin, or Greek—a phrase destined to express some one's influence on some one else, with the intervention and co-operation of a third person, where the preposition 'in' would be aptly employed to convey the mode of that third person's intervention or co-operation. I may feel most anxious about the moral conduct of a favourite brother of mine. No concern in the world is nearer to my heart than his salvation from ruin. There is one redeeming point in him. He is fond of our common sister, a paragon of virtue and love. In her is all my hope. Both for my sake and her own she follows the scapegrace, she wins him back through her masterful delicacy. No words could describe what my gratitude to her really is. I feel that she has made this salvation possible; yet my speech would be foolish if I said that I saved my brother 'in' her. I saved him through her, I say, and more I could not say.

Yet St. Paul prefers the first form of speech. God saves me not through His Son, but in His Son. It is not merely an idiosyncrasy of St. Paul's style—in fact, the idiosyncrasy would hardly be short of a barbarism—it is a necessity of St. Paul's theology. Let us take as an instance St. Paul's magnificent passage in the second chapter of the Epistle to the Ephesians. I keep the prepositions as they are in the Greek text. 'But God who is rich in mercy, for his exceeding charity wherewith he loved us, even when we were dead in sins, hath quickened us together in Christ, by whose grace you are saved; and hath raised us up together, and hath made us sit together in the heavenly places in Christ Jesus, that he might show in the ages to come the abundant riches of his grace, in his bounty towards us in Christ Jesus. . . . For we are his workmanship created in Christ Jesus in good works, which God hath prepared that we should walk in them.'

The most remarkable association of words in this most remarkable passage is the verse : ' And he hath made us sit together in the heavenly places in Christ Jesus.' The Douai translator for one found the reduplication of the ' in ' too much for him, and he calmly translates ' in the heavenly places through Christ.' In fact, in ordinary grammar the phrase would sound ludicrous ; but nowhere do we find St. Paul guilty of a careless use of prepositions. He distinguishes carefully between the preposition of instrumentality and the preposition that marks inclusion. Note, for instance, his phrase :[1] ' For if you have ten thousand instructors in Christ, yet not many fathers. For in Christ Jesus by the Gospel I have begotten you.' The Greek and the Latin discriminate clearly between the two propositions. The constant use of the unwonted term ' in ' simply points to a spiritual truth, clearly perceived by St. Paul, and for which no doubt there is no received phraseology in

[1] 1 Cor. iv. 15.

the ordinary language. Christ's co-operation with God in the sanctification of the elect is expressed almost invariably by St. Paul, not as an action of God through Him, but as an action of God in Him. 'For God indeed was in Christ reconciling the world to himself.'[1] The action of God is confined within Christ's Personality, and making Him what He is, is God's way of saving and sanctifying the human race. 'In whom all the building fitly framed together groweth unto an holy temple in the Lord.'[2]

[1] 2 Cor. v. 19.   [2] Eph. ii. 21.

CHAPTER XVII

CHRIST ALL IN ALL

INTELLECTUAL and philosophical ages are the high-water mark of human progress. They come and go with their blessings and dangers, as all the other manifestations of the activities of progressive humanity come and go, according to unknown rules, almost with the regularity of the ocean tides.

One of the blessings of a philosophical age is of course the love for the 'universal,' for what is beyond the narrow limits of time and space. An unphilosophical, a positive and materialistic age has no love except for the particular fact, the thing that has avoirdupois and the thing that can be measured by an equivalent in hard cash. But this very love for the universal, which is the trait of a thinking generation, has its dangers: it leads to various forms of thought, to various 'isms'—the expression has become common enough to be used without an air of pretence—before which there stands the dangerous Greek prefix 'pan.'

Pantheism, for one thing, is the most common intellectual sin in a philosophical age. The philosophical temper likes oneness in all things. We are all one God, we are all one Mind, we are all one Spirit, says the philosophical mind that has the defects of its qualities, an excessive love for the universal.

May I be forgiven for coining an expression that represents a good deal of undefined thinking and feeling in our times—times in which the drift of human evolution sets in the direction of philosophical thought. May I be permitted to speak of 'pan-christism.' We are all Christ's, we are all instances of the Incarnation; we are all sons of God; there is a Christ within us all, etc. Phrases of similar import are as common in the writings and speeches of religious men of our own days as the criticisms of the day's weather are common in daily social intercourse.

The aberration is the defect of a great quality, the shadow cast by a great light : men are reluctant to make of a person quite outside themselves the principle of their higher life, though that person be of surpassing excellency. The very fact of 'outsideness' puts even the very personification of human excellency at a disadvantage, with regard to our own intimate life, if that personification be a concrete individual. At bottom, all pantheistic and all 'pan-christic' tendencies come from this deep-rooted aversion of the spiritually minded to make of an isolated individuality the principle of one's most intimate life.

Against pantheism Christianity has the indwelling of the Holy Ghost, that great spiritual fact which brings man nearer to God than pantheism itself, as through it man is not only near God but above himself—above the potentialities of the plane of his own nature, an elevation quite unthinkable in the metaphysics of ordinary pantheism, where man is divine through the laws of his own spirit, and where therefore, logically, ascent is impossible, as man already is part of the Deity. If Christianity had no such spiritual fact as the indwelling of the Holy Ghost in the human soul, its fight with pantheism would have a poor outlook. Modern pan-christism is born from a narrowing of Christ's spiritual position. Let us give Christ the position of traditional Catholic theology, and we shall find in Him the life-giving principle of what is highest in us; we shall find Him at the very root of our being, and yet we shall not feel tempted to break down the barriers of His wonderful individuality, with a view to making Him less personal and more communicable to us. One thing I may note here. Pan-christism is a modern form of aberration. It comes from a lingering faith in, and love for, Christ, unsustained by deep Christology.

Our theology of Christ is not like a tale with a

purpose, written just with a view to refute or redress or silence an error. Catholic and scholastic Christology received its completion long before the tendencies I call pan-christism. Yet such as Catholic Christianity is to-day, it is to pan-christism what the indwelling of the Holy Ghost is to pantheism—its cure, its refutation, and, above all, its higher and healthier substitute.

A literal interpretation of many of Christ's utterances points decidedly to the universal relationship of His person with the human race.

'Father, the hour is come; glorify the Son, that thy Son may glorify thee: as thou hast given him power over all flesh, that he may give eternal life to all whom thou hast given him.' [1]

'My Father worketh until now, and I work. Hereupon therefore the Jews sought the more to kill him, because he did not only break the sabbath, but also said God was his Father, making himself equal to God. Then Jesus answered and said to them, Amen, Amen, I say unto you, The Son cannot do anything of himself, but what he seeth the Father doing; for what things soever he doth, them the Son also doth in like manner. For the Father loveth the Son, and sheweth him all things which himself doth, and greater works than these will he shew him, that you may wonder. For as the Father raiseth up the dead, and giveth life;

[1] St. John xvii. 1, 2.

so also the Son giveth life to whom he will. For neither doth the Father judge any man, but hath given all judgment to the Son: that all men may honour the Son, as they honour the Father. He who honoureth not the Son honoureth not the Father who hath sent him. . . . For as the Father hath life in himself, so he hath given to the Son also to have life in himself: and he hath given him power to do judgment, because he is the Son of man.'[1]

'Now this is the will of my Father that sent me, that every one who seeth the Son, and believeth in him, may have life everlasting, and I will raise him up in the last day. . . . The bread that I will give is my flesh for the life of the World.'[2]

It would be easy to multiply quotations that would establish beyond doubt the fact that Christ constantly attributes to Himself not only a universality of relationship with the human race, but a relationship of life, a relationship of light, He being to all men of good will what is most subjective in man, spiritual life and spiritual light.

This filling up of creation by Christ is a cherished idea with St. Paul in the Epistle to the Ephesians. 'He [God] hath subjected all things under his [Christ's] feet: and hath made him head over all the Church, which is his body, and the fulness of

[1] St. John v. 17 *seq.*   [2] St. John vi. 40, 51.

him, who is filled all in all.'[1] 'To know also the charity of Christ, which surpasseth all knowledge, that you may be filled unto all the fulness of God.'[2] 'He [Christ] that descended is the same also that ascended above all the heavens, that he might fill all things. . . . Until we all meet into the unity of faith, and of the knowledge of the Son of God, unto a perfect man, unto the measure of the age of the fulness of Christ.'[3]

This idea of fulness stands for the greatest spiritual facts in the New Testament. 'And of his fulness we all have received, and grace for grace.'[4] 'For in him [Christ] dwelleth the fulness of the Godhead corporally.'[5] Consummate sanctity is to be filled with the Holy Ghost in the language of the New Testament.

When therefore we see Christ spoken of so insistently as a filling up of the capacities of the spiritual world, we are confronted by a spiritual fact of the highest importance—a fact as great as the filling up of the human heart by the Holy Ghost, a fact that is the parallel of that fulness of the indwelling of Divinity in Christ Himself. If there is the indwelling of the Spirit of God in man, there is also the indwelling of Christ in man's heart. 'That Christ may dwell by faith in your hearts'[6] is a saying as pregnant with the realities

---
[1] Eph. i. 22, 23. [2] Eph. iii. 19. [3] Eph. iv. 10, 13.
[4] St. John i. 16. [5] Col. ii. 9. [6] Eph. iii. 17.

of true spiritual immanence as that other phrase: 'Know you not that you are the temple of God, and that the Spirit of God dwelleth in you?'[1]

There is nothing left that a mystical lover of Christ could desire in the way of oneness with Him than that such phraseology should be taken literally. Christ's lover may not possess the theological training that enables the mind to conceive psychic possibilities of such a nature as will make the literal interpretation of the texts the most obvious interpretation; but his spiritual instinct will all be in favour of as intimate an indwelling of Christ in the human race as possible. The idea of the 'fulness' is for his mystical powers; the idea of the *instrumentum conjunctum Divinitatis* is for his reasoning powers. The two ideas complete each other.

'As thou hast sent me into the world, I also have sent them into the world. And for them do I sanctify myself, that they also may be sanctified in truth. And not for them only do I pray, but for them also who through their word shall believe in me; that they all may be one, as thou Father, in me, and I in thee, that they also may be one in us · that the world may believe that thou hast sent me. And the glory which thou hast given me I have given to them; that they may be one, as we also are one; I in them, and thou

[1] 1 Cor. iii. 16.

CHRIST ALL IN ALL

in me, that they may be made perfect in one: and the world may know that thou hast sent me.

' As thou hast sent me into the world, I also have sent them into the world.' [1]

The Pauline idea of God's merciful operations taking place within Christ's personality, deep as it is, is not deeper than the Johannine view expressed in this passage. St. John states most unequivocally the doctrine of our being Christ's fulness, the doctrine of the *pleroma*; for such is the Greek for it.

I do not think that we could find anywhere in the scriptures words more pregnant with mystical significance of the highest order, and words more illuminating as to the real meaning of our being sanctified in Christ, and our being the ' filling up ' the *pleroma* of Christ.

In the Epistle to the Colossians chapter ii., we find St. Paul making the same juxtaposition of that double presence in Christ, the presence of God and the presence in Him of the Elect. ' For in him dwelleth all the fulness of the Godhead, corporally; and you are filled in him, who is the head of all principality and power.' ' I in them, and thou in me '; such is the double filling up constituted by the mystery of the Incarnation.

The *pleroma* is essentially a glory that is inside Christ, not outside Him. The first chapter

---

[1] St. John xvii. 18, *seq.*

to the Colossians makes this perfectly clear. After saying that Christ is the image of the unseen God, that all the heavenly powers are created in Him, are kept together in Him, that He is the head of the Church, the Apostle says,' Because in him it has well pleased (the father) that all fulness should dwell.' This indwelling of the *pleroma* in Him is the reason of the Divine, Angelic, and Church orders being united in Him. Christ therefore has a threefold *pleroma*, and all three dwell within Him.

The second and third, the Church *pleroma*, interact, i.e. Christ's fills up the angelic world and the Church, and He is filled up by them. His dwelling in a created spirit is the created spirit's dwelling in Him. 'He that eateth my flesh and drinketh my blood abideth in me, and I in him. As the living father hath sent me, and I live by the father; so he that eateth me, the same also shall live by me.' [1]

This mutuality of indwelling between Christ and His elect is clearly a New Testament idea.

In Eph. i. 23 Christ is said to be filled up all in all, passively. In Eph. iv. 10 Christ is said actively to fill up all things. Finally, in Col. ii. 10 the faithful are said to be filled up in Him, passively. In the light of that mutuality of indwelling, so clearly stated in St. John's Gospel, these various

[1] St. John vi. 56, 57.

CHRIST ALL IN ALL

modes of speech easily point to the same spiritual reality, a great compenetration between Christ and the Elect.

Another parallelism worth remarking is found in St. Paul's expression in 1 Cor. xv. 28, where he describes the consummation of all things after the Resurrection, when God will be all things in all. 'That God may be all in all.' Now this phrase 'all in all' is used with regard to Christ as a predicate in Eph. i. 23; only instead of saying that Christ is all in all, St. Paul says that He is filled all in all.

'And when all things shall be subjected unto him [Christ], then the Son also himself shall be subjected unto him that put all things under him, that God may be all in all.'[1] This is the formula for the true pantheism of Christianity. 'And he [the Father] hath subjected all things under his feet, and hath made him head over all the church, which is his body, and the fulness of him who is filled all in all.'[2] This is our true and most consoling pan-christism.

[1] 1 Cor. xv. 28.   [2] Eph. i. 22, 23.

CHAPTER XVIII

CHRIST'S RESERVES

It may be a practical difficulty to many minds to find happiness in that hierarchy of sublimities that constitute the God-man, as such a hierarchy with its division of glories and attributes may not be conducive to love; yet the mystery of Christ ought to be the sweetest of all mysteries. It has therefore occurred to me that the hierarchical gradation of sanctities and glories in Christ could be best expressed through the English word 'reserve'; they are so many reserves of graces and glories that make Christ's Personality so intensely attractive.

When we are in contact with people whom we believe to be possessed of high moral or intellectual qualities, who have done brave deeds or said wise things, the daily ordinary intercourse with them has wonderful charm, owing to our impression that there is a great reserve of superior power in them. Most of our intercourse is of the ordinary character, yet all along we feel that there is something higher, and this latent conviction lends additional charm to the daily urbanities.

This is the kind of simile I would fain propose to those that approach the Son of God. He is the Son of man. He is a perfect man; you will find in Him all the charms of perfect humanity. Go deep into that humanity and love it tenderly; very soon you will find that behind the humanity there is a wonderful reserve of grace that is more than human. You feel its presence, though it may not act directly; but there is such a majesty in that humanity as to make it clear that the humanity is passing into something more than human. If that superhuman element is approached, there again it is such as to point to a tremendous reserve behind it. There is the Divine Personality deeply concealed underneath the created glories and graces, and lending them that infinitude of vista and possibility which it is so refreshing for the created spirit to catch a glimpse of. Christ's glorious finitudes sweetly and gradually are merged into the infinitudes of His Divine Personality. We enter into Him as man, His humanity is the door, we go out of His Humanity into His angelic life, into His divine life, and our mind finds indeed its pasture in Him. 'I am the door: by me if any man enter in, he shall be saved, he shall go in and go out, and shall find pastures.'[1]

[1] St. John x. 9.

124 THE PERSONALITY OF CHRIST

Nothing could be more refreshing than to read St. John's Gospel in the light of this idea of reserve. The Jewish mind is puzzled, is irritated with this wonderful personality of Christ. They cannot make him out; they quarrel amongst themselves about Him; they feel, in spite of themselves, that there is something extraordinary behind His human appearance. It is not only His miracles that are extraordinary, His whole personality is an enigma. His enemies, in true Jewish fashion, have a ready explanation for this incomprehensible masterfulness of the hated Rabbi. He has within Himself an evil spirit. 'The Jews therefore answered and said to him, Do we not say well that thou art a Samaritan, and hast a devil? . . . Now we know that thou hast a devil. Abraham is dead, and the prophets; and thou sayest, If any man keep my word he shall not taste death for ever. Art thou greater than our Father Abraham, who is dead?'[1]

But a dissension arose again among the Jews for these words, 'And many of them said, He has a devil, and is mad; why hear you him? Others said, These are not the words of one who hath a devil. Can a devil open the eyes of the blind?'[2]

The Gospel of St. John is in fact full of assertions on Christ's part as to the presence in Him of glories that do not appear to the eye. 'Amen, Amen, I say to thee that we speak what we know,

[1] St. John viii. 48-53.   [2] St. John x. 19-21.

and we testify what we have seen; and you receive not our testimony. If I had spoken to you earthly things, and you believed not, how will you believe if I shall speak to you heavenly things, and no man has ascended into heaven but he that descendeth from heaven, the Son of man who is in heaven.'[1]

It might be said without exaggeration that the whole trend of Christ's discourses, as well as the Baptist's testimony in the fourth Gospel, is this: there is more in this man than appears to the eye; even His miracles, great as they are, do not give the measure of His greatness; but they entitle Him to be listened to even when He says that He and the Father are one. Quotations to that effect could be multiplied so as to make of the chapter a kind of *résumé* of St. John's Gospel. A few more must suffice. 'And it was the feast of the dedication at Jerusalem, and it was winter. And Jesus walked in the Temple in Solomon's porch. The Jews therefore came round about Him, and said to Him, How long dost thou hold our souls in suspense? If thou be the Christ, tell us plainly. Jesus answered them, I speak to you, and you believe not; the works that I do in the name of My Father, they give testimony of me. . . .

'I and the Father are one. The Jews then took up stones to stone Him. Jesus answered them: Many good works I have shewn you from

[1] St. John iii. 11-13.

my Father; for which of those works do you stone me? The Jews answered Him, For a good work we stone thee not, but for the blasphemy; and because that thou, being a man, makest thyself God. Jesus answered them, Is it not written in your law, I said, You are gods? If he called them gods, to whom the word of God was spoken (and the scripture cannot be broken), do you say of him, whom the Father hath sanctified, and sent into the world, Thou blasphemest; because I said I am the Son of God? If I do not the works of my Father, believe me not. But if I do, though you will not believe me, believe the works; that you may know, and believe, that the Father is in me, and I in the Father. They sought therefore to take him, and he escaped out of their hands.'

One cannot resist quoting once more. From the fierce antagonism of the Pharisee let us come to the good-natured perplexity of the disciples themselves, of Philip, the ingenious questioner in the Gospel, and let us hear the divine answer given with wonderful playfulness. 'If you had known me, you would without doubt have known my Father also; and from henceforth you shall know him, and you have seen him. Philip saith to him: Lord, shew us the Father, and it is enough for us. Jesus saith to him: So long a time have I been with you, and have you not known me? Philip, he that seeth me, seeth the Father also

How sayest thou, Shew us the Father? Do you not believe that I am in the Father, and the Father in me? The words that I speak to you I speak not of myself: but the Father who abideth in me, he doth the works. Believe you not that I am in the Father, and the Father in me?'

CHAPTER XIX

THE HIDING OF CHRIST'S GODHEAD

In our chapter entitled 'Reserve' we have tried to give of Christ's complex Personality such a view as to make contemplation of Him a sweet and gradual ascent from winsomeness unto winsomeness within that human nature in which, according to St. Paul, Godhead had taken up a bodily abode. 'For in him dwelleth all the fulness of the Godhead, corporally.'[1]

There is one theological truth which is of importance, if we are to relish the mystery of Christ, and the truth is this: Though Christ's Personality be an ever-ascending succession of spiritual sublimities, there was during His mortal life a check put on those sublimities by God's omnipotence, lest through the presence in Christ's soul of such marvellous vitalities, Christ's soul should not be a sharer in our common state of mortality.

St. Thomas, always so reluctant to admit exceptional interposition of God's providence, is

[1] Col. ii. 9.

compelled to confess that God prevented the higher graces in the soul of Christ, such as Beatific Vision, from making themselves felt within Christ's soul according to their full possibilities.

It is evident that the presence of such a gift as the clear vision of God within a human spirit by ordinary law ought to dispel any cloud of sadness from that spirit. To see God face to face as Christ saw Him is a happiness so intense as to raise the subject's soul and body above the sphere of sorrow and suffering.

Yet Christ was sorrowful in the deepest and holiest regions of His soul. He suffered in His body, He suffered in every one of His mental faculties. We are therefore to admit a psychological miracle in Christ, the only psychological miracle within Him known to theology. It is a miracle of wonderful subtlety, showing clearly what possibilities there must be in the human soul. Beatific Vision and the other spiritual sublimities were all there, in full activity; all the treasures of wisdom and knowledge were within His intellect. ' In whom are hid all the treasures of wisdom and knowledge.' [1]

And yet by a direct intervention of God, as St. Thomas says, they did not flow over; they were kept back from certain regions of Christ's soul, from certain powers of Christ's body, in order that

[1] Col. ii. 3.

Christ should have power to suffer and to merit, to be sorrowful and to be fearful for the redeemed.

It was a psychological miracle because it was the suspension of effects that should naturally have followed, and I say that it is the only miracle in Christ's Person; His Person as such is not exactly a miracle, it is a wonder, the greatest of all wonders; but it is not the suspension of any laws, it is, on the contrary, the application of the highest laws of God's power, whilst a miracle always implies a suspension of a result that ought to be.

The modern rationalist may find it difficult to see in the Jesus of Nazareth, who was obedient to His parents, the Christ of St. Paul such as He is described in the Epistles to the Ephesians and the Colossians, though, as a matter of history, the aforesaid Epistles were written before the Gospel of St. Luke. We admit that without a direct miracle the Christ in whom all the fulness was pleased to dwell, 'Because in him it hath well pleased the Father that all fulness should dwell,' could not have been the boy who sat among the doctors at the age of twelve, asking questions and receiving answers from them. There was in Him another kind of reserve, taking reserve now in its active meaning; there was a miraculous keeping back from certain regions of His Personality of the glories of His Godhead.

This is what is meant by the constant theological expression that Christ was at the same time *compre-*

THE HIDING OF CHRIST'S GODHEAD

hensor and *viator*—that is to say, a seer of God and a wayfarer, a pilgrim abroad and a guest in the Father's house. 'And no man hath ascended into heaven but he that descendeth from heaven, the Son of man who is in heaven.'[1] He was at the same time full of the eternal life and subject to the agonies of human death; the highest regions of His soul were thrilled with the joys of the Blessed Vision, and those same regions were saddened with the sight of the world's iniquities; for it would not be generous to think of our Lord's soul having happiness in its highest faculties and sorrow merely in its lower powers. His sorrow was a divine sorrow, as it was sorrow for the creature's theological guilt; as such, it had to be in the noblest part of His soul, where there was the thrill of Beatific Vision.

But such division of soul and spirit, such blending of light and darkness, is a miracle, and, as I have said, it is only the abnormal thing in Christ's Personality. The abnormality ceased when He gave up His soul to the Father on the cross.

[1] St. John iii. 13.

CHAPTER XX

THE FORM OF THE SLAVE

CHRIST'S attitude towards physical and mental suffering is of immense practical significance for man's daily life, as well as for the progress of civilisation. We are far to-day from the times that admired a nature ' red in tooth and claw,' and it becomes a very pressing question on the Christian theologian how the wonderful victories over physical pain won by modern science are in line with the gospel of the Cross.

I think it profitable to my patient reader to give him an exhaustive rendering of the theological teaching concerning Christ's attitude towards pain and suffering. Morbidness, even *in excelsis*, is unforgiveable, and it is perhaps all the more deleterious to healthy soul-life because it is stretched into infinitude.

By Christ's body we mean of course the whole extent of Christ's sensitive life, which, more than any other human life, is a wonderful summary of all that is beautiful in the physical world. No human intellect can fathom the possibilities of an organism vivified and elevated by a soul so perfect as was Christ's soul. That suffering and death should enter into such an organism is a thought more appalling than that sin should have been found in the angels of God. It is only our familiarity with the mystery of the Cross that makes us look on Christ's sufferings as on an obvious natural phenomenon.

The wondering compassion of the saints who are overawed and stirred in their souls with the thought that God suffered is by no means a misplaced sentiment. For Christ, in His Humanity, was entitled, by all the laws of the Hypostatic Union, to an absolutely divine immunity from pain and suffering. Divinity itself could never be subject to any kind of suffering whatsoever. It would be the worst of all blasphemies to say that God, in His own life, could experience any contrariety. No created gain could come from the Creator's loss, as there is nothing so profitable to the finite being as that infinitude should inhabit the region of unassailable bliss, to which every creature may tend as to the unalterable felicity. With Divinity, suffering is an absolute contradiction in terms, both from the point of view of God's life and God's sanctity. A strong God, as well as a holy God, is infinitely above every thinkable sort of disappointment. Now this aloofness from sorrow is Christ's natural condition from the very laws of

Hypostatic Union. The divinity of Christ's person is in itself such an exemption from the ordinary laws of mortality that no exclamation of surprise on the lips of the lover of Jesus at seeing Him suffer and die can be too strong.

Theology starts with the assertion that Christ's normal condition would have been unassailable bliss of mind and invulnerable glory of body; that both mind and body in Him should have become a prey to pain and sorrow and death is the result of a miracle. Through an act of His omnipotence, Christ in His own person suspended the natural law of Hypostatic Union, the law that makes complete bliss of mind the immortality of the body. Through the fact of Hypostatic Union Christ's human mind was endowed, from the very first moment of its own self-consciousness, with the clear vision of God, commonly called Beatific Vision. Now, such a completeness of blissful contemplation brings with itself a quickening and a glorifying of the whole bodily organism, such as theology teaches will take place in the glorious resurrection of the elect at the end of the world. A glorified mind—that is to say, a mind under Beatific Vision—means a glorified body, by a natural concomitance or causality, which theologians call *redundantia*—a flowing over of the higher bliss into the lower powers. This *redundantia* is a natural psychological law.

With Christ, or rather in Christ, this law was

miraculously suspended by His own omnipotence. The term 'miracle' taken technically is not too strong to describe this great spiritual anomaly in Christ's Personality. A miracle is a suspension of the results of the ordinary laws, either material or spiritual, by a direct divine interposition. Fire, whilst remaining fire and keeping its activity, and yet not burning a naturally combustible object within its range, is a miracle. Both the fire and the combustible object must remain in their native state in order that there should be a suspension of laws. If divine omnipotence changed, say, the nature of the combustible to make it fireproof, there would be no suspension of laws; it would not be the kind of miracle that would need necessarily divine omnipotence. My reader will readily forgive my digression if I remind him of my aim in all this: Christ's immunity, by birthright, from suffering. Such was His immunity that the suspension of that immunity belongs to the class of miraculous effects best instanced by fire and straw keeping their respective properties and not burning when brought into contact.

Nothing but such faith in Christ's immunity could make us grasp the meaning of scriptural expressions like the one in St. Paul's Epistle to the Philippians, chapter ii.

'For let this mind be in you, which was also in Christ Jesus: who, being in the form of God, thought it not robbery to be equal with God : but emptied himself, taking the form of a servant, being made in the likeness of men, and in habit found as a man. He humbled himself, becoming obedient unto death, even the death of the cross.'

All the humiliation and abasement of the Incarnation lie in this doctrine. The union of the Second Person of the Trinity, with a finite created nature, could never be considered as the 'humiliation.' It is, on the contrary, one of the masterpieces of God's omnipotence. Moreover, Divinity itself could not be 'abased' without infinite loss to the whole creation, besides its being inherently impossible, as I have said already. But that Christ should appear under the form of a servant, as slave, was indeed humiliation, and abasement inconceivably great. The Risen Christ, the Christ of to-day, has no shadow of humiliation. Hypostatic Union with a glorified human nature, such as was postulated by the very laws of Christ's Beatific Vision would have lacked completely the element of humiliation.

I now quote St. Thomas himself, stating the great psychological miracle inside Christ's Person. 'By the power of His Divinity, as a special dispensation (*dispensative*), bliss was thus kept back in the soul, that it did not flow down into the body, lest the power of suffering and of dying should be taken away from Him. And in the same way the delights of the vision were thus pent up in His mind, that nothing of these went down to the sensitive powers, lest by that sense-suffering should be rendered impossible.'[1]

The best paraphrase on this very tersely put doctrine is given by Cajetan, when he comments on the doctrine of St. Thomas on Christ's Transfiguration.[2] So persistent are the views of those great thinkers as to the miraculous nature of Christ's passibleness, that Cajetan, in speaking of the momentary glory of Christ's body in the Transfiguration, considers such a manifestation a new miracle, because the first miracle—the miracle of the suspension—was to be of so permanent a character that its cessation for a moment meant another interference on the part of Omnipotence. ' Let us grant therefore that both phenomena were miraculous ; I mean that Christ's body should not shine (with glory), and that it shone thus in the Transfiguration. But the former is part of the first and, so to say; universal and old (*antiquum*) miracle that took place in the Incarnation, by which was suspended that communication of glory from the Soul to the Body of Christ, in order that He might have a passible body. . . . The latter phenomenon belongs to a special miracle, by which was granted that moment, to the passible body, the power of shining.'

[1] Quest. 15, art. 5, ad 3 m.   [2] Quest. 45, art. 2.

After establishing the principles of Christ's natural immunity from suffering, and of His natural right to highest beatific bliss of soul and body, our theology inquires how much of human pain and sadness Christ took upon Himself. For the miraculous suspension was anything but a wanton courting of human misery. That He should take as much and no more than was necessary for the aim of His Incarnation is to be taken for granted, on the principle that He acted with consummate wisdom and prudence in everything, as He is the Incarnate Wisdom of God.

In the fourth article of question 14 St. Thomas has an exhaustive study as to the kind of human infirmities and passibilities which it was fit for Christ to take upon Himself. The ruling principle is the raising up of the human race through the Incarnation. Only such infirmities were to be assumed which were co-extensive with the race itself, and whose healing in Christ would affect the healing of the whole race. Infirmities that come from private causes, not universal racial causes, Christ had not to take upon Himself. St. Thomas quotes hunger and thirst and death as racial infirmities. Other infirmities called illness are not racial; they come from particular causes. However vast those causes may be, they are not universal and co-extensive with the race itself.

No doubt it would be difficult, at this time of

THE FORM OF THE SLAVE 139

the day, to say what limitations in our bodily well-being are racial, and what are of less comprehensive an origin. No doubt a human organism with just the racial limitations in it, without any vestige of decadence that comes from heredity, would be a marvellous fount of life. Yet, in strict theology, Christ's body was such. His own personal wisdom and moderation of life made any suffering that comes from an ignorance of the art of life absolutely unthinkable. It is practically impossible for us to grasp what a supremely refined life Christ's was, from this absence of any hereditary taint. His body had been fashioned by the Holy Ghost Himself from a stainless human blood. Moreover, as St. Thomas points out in this same article, as fulness of grace and wisdom was as necessary to the work of the Incarnation as suffering, Christ could never have allowed in Himself any defect that would have interfered in the least with such a perfection of holiness and knowledge : there was no ignorance in Him, no mental tardiness, no contradiction between the higher and the lower powers. Though such defects may be racial in their extent, yet Christ took exception to them, as they are in opposition to consummate sanctity.

We owe great thanks to our theology for having kept our Christ in this serene height of bodily purity and health, for having made it possible for us to find in Him at the same time the most perfect example of patience in pain and suffering, as well as the undying fount of spiritual and bodily health.

It is evident from all this that nothing is less in conformity with the Christ idea than the accumulation of hereditary infirmities that weigh down mankind. Christ banished them from His own body; so it is a Christian policy, so to speak, to banish them from the human race to any extent human means may allow.

On the other hand, when such infirmities have taken hold on us, their patient endurance becomes closely allied with Christ's patience on the cross. For though He did not take such infirmities on Himself, He willingly took those older and more universal infirmities that are the parents of newer forms of suffering.

To a suggestion that it would have been more generous of Christ to take on Himself every kind of human weakness, in order to heal them all, St. Thomas answers: 'To the first objection I answer that all particular defects in men are caused by the corruptibility and passibility of the body, with the addition of certain particular causes. And therefore as Christ healed the passibility and corruptibility of our body by the very fact of taking them on Himself, as a consequence He has healed all the other defects.'[1]

Christ's body is a source of life through its

[1] Quest. 14, Art. 4.

THE FORM OF THE SLAVE

matchless perfection of nature and grace. St. Thomas insists frequently on the causes of this most heavenly temperament of Christ's bodily frame : the active generative cause and the passive material element. The Holy Ghost Himself is the first, and Mary's most pure blood is the second, of the two total causes of our Lord's human body. Who can tell the riches of health and life and grace hidden in an organism of such origin ? Significantly St. Thomas teaches in article two of the eighth question that Christ is the head of men both through His soul and His body. ' Therefore the whole humanity of Christ—that is to say both according to (His) soul and (His) body—exerts an influence on men, both with regard to (their) soul and with regard to (their) body.

CHAPTER XXI

THE TRANSITION

CHRIST'S passing at the age of thirty from ordinary human life into one of power, claiming to be that of the Son of God, was abrupt and unexpected. Nothing in His daily existence had prepared His townsmen for this sudden exchange of rôles. That He was the village carpenter is evident from the phrase on the lips of the people of Nazareth, quoted by St. Mark. 'And when the sabbath was come, he began to teach in the synagogue: and many hearing him were in admiration at his doctrine, saying, How came this man by all these things? and what wisdom is this that is given to him, and such mighty works as are wrought by his hands? Is not this the carpenter, the son of Mary, the brother of James, and Joseph, and Jude, and Simon? Are not also his sisters here with us? And they were scandalised in regard of him.'[1]

St. Joseph was dead, and Jesus had succeeded to his foster-father's modest business. St. Matt. xiii. 55 makes the people of Nazareth say: 'Is not this

[1] Mark vi. 2, 3.

the carpenter's son?' whilst St. Mark's text points clearly to the fact that Jesus Himself had followed the parental avocation.

Adam Bede has become the classical instance, in English literature, of the noble son of the soil, grand in his simple manhood, for whom it was God's will that he should be a good carpenter. There is no profaneness in thinking of Christ, at Nazareth, going about His work in the simple uprightness of a strong and straightforward man, to whom the great secrets of His spiritual life were never a temptation even to look mysterious and secretive.

The Gospel narratives are documents of supreme good taste. The element of useless mysteriousness, of irritating secretiveness is entirely banished from them. The apocrypha, on the contrary, exploit bravely this situation, so full of possible thrills for the vulgar mind, a human being that is a God, and yet of set purpose hiding his identity, with just enough hints and glimpses given to the entourage to make the situation interesting, till finally the veil falls.

No human being ever possessed the noble quality of reserve in the degree it was possessed by the divine carpenter, the son of David.

But when the hour of His manifestation came, it came with incontrovertible clearness and irresistible power. It came as an immense surprise to

Christ's friends and acquaintances. In their bewilderment they had the one explanation always at hand for nonplussed family circles, sudden insanity. 'And when his friends had heard of it, they went out to lay hold on him : for they said, He is become mad.'[1]

The Baptism at the hands of John and the great fast with its mysterious temptations were events still unknown to the world. John alone had seen the open heaven, had heard the voice from above. The calling of the first disciples, with such irresistible imperiousness of will, was Christ's first assertion of His Divinity. A few days later there was the miracle at Cana, the first sign. From that day Christ's progress was rapid and overpowering, so that He could not openly go into the city, but was without in desert places ; and they flocked to Him from all sides. 'But he being gone out, began to publish and to blaze abroad the word ; so that he could not openly go into the city, but was without in desert places : and they flocked to him from all sides.'[2] The hatred of the Pharisaical body and their conspiracy to destroy Him are events that already belong to the first months of Christ's public appearance. 'And the Pharisees going out, immediately made a consultation with the Herodians against him, how they might destroy him.'[3]

[1] Mark iii. 21.   [2] Mark i. 45.   [3] Mark iii. 6.

THE TRANSITION

The abruptness of this transition from the normal human existence into an all-bewildering manifestation of superhuman powers, whilst perfectly compatible with the principles of Hypostatic Union, contradicts any theory that makes of Christ's ascendancy the gradual evolution of a saintly life and superior personality.

Jewish tradition, the outcome of the Jewish love for the marvellous and mysterious, was all in favour of a Christ whose origin would be wrapped up in impenetrable mystery. 'And behold he speaketh openly, and they say nothing to him. Have the rulers known for a truth that this is the Christ. But we know this man whence he is: but when the Christ cometh, no man knoweth whence he is.'[1]

No prophet's home life and early upbringing were so clearly known as Christ's. 'Jesus therefore cried out in the temple, teaching and saying, You both know me, and you know whence I am; but I am not come of myself; but he that sent me is true, whom ye know not.'[2] Everybody in Jerusalem knew that He belonged to the class of the illiterate. 'And the Jews wondered, saying, How doth this man know letters, having never learned?'[3] The sudden reputation of the young teacher had no doubt produced a great eagerness and curiosity as

---

[1] St. John vii. 26, 27.   [2] St. John vii. 28.
[3] St. John vii. 15.

to his antecedents. But there was nothing to learn, nothing to marvel at. The most ordinary, the most uneventful, past was the only thing that met the gaze of the inquisitive busybody.

No religion indeed aims so little at the marvellous for its own sake as the religion of Christ. ' Ordinariness ' of condition is the rule, and there is no limit as to the spiritual worth that may be found within this ordinariness of the conditions of human existence.

It is precisely this complete ordinariness of His previous life that was the great stumbling-block to the Jewish mind. The greatest miracles seemed powerless to efface that first fact. The men of Nazareth were scandalised in regard of Him. ' Is not this the carpenter, the son of Mary, the brother of James, and Joseph, and Jude, and Simon ? Are not also his sisters here with us ? And they were scandalised in regard of him.' [1]

' And when the men were come unto him, they said, John the Baptist hath sent us to thee, saying : Art thou he that art to come, or look we for another ? (And in that same hour he cured many of their diseases, and hurts, and evil spirits ; and to many that were blind he gave sight.) And answering, he said to them, Go and relate to John what you have heard and seen ; the blind see, the lame walk, the lepers are made clean, the deaf hear, the

[1] Mark vi. 3.

dead rise again, to the poor the gospel is preached : And blessed is he whosoever shall not be scandalised in me.'[1] This last verse seems a strange conclusion to that enumeration of miraculous deeds of the highest order, such as the raising up of the dead. But it finds its natural commentary in the analogous passage of St. Mark, where Christ's nearest acquaintances are said to have been scandalised with regard to Him, though they admitted the fact of the 'mighty works' as 'wrought by his hands.' All this goes to show how completely Christ took His countrymen by surprise when He began to 'manifest His glory.'[2]

Christ had His 'hour.' 'And Jesus saith to her : Woman what is that to me and to thee ? my hour is not yet come.'[3] Before that hour had come, no power in the world, except the prayers of His mother, could open His lips, or get Him to reveal the ineffable secret of His Personality. But when He thought that the hour had come, the secret unburdened itself from His breast with the rush of a mighty stream.

This complete mastery of Christ over His own feelings, His own destiny, expressed in the term 'my hour,' is a cherished idea in the Gospel of St. John. Besides the passages just quoted, where it refers to the great transition from obscurity to Divinity, it marks other new phases of Christ's

[1] Luke vii. 20-23.   [2] St. John ii. 11.   [3] St. John ii. 4.

career. 'They sought therefore to apprehend him: and no man laid hands on him, because his hour was not yet come.'[1] 'These words Jesus spoke in the treasury, teaching in the temple and no man laid hands on him, because his hour was not yet come.'[2] 'But Jesus answered them, saying: The hour is come, that the Son of Man should be glorified.'[3] 'Before the festival day of the pasch, Jesus knowing that his hour was come, that he should pass out of this world to the Father, having loved his own who were in the world, he loved them unto the end.'[4]

There is an apparent contradiction in the Gospels in this matter of Christ's manifestation. His birth was surrounded with the elements of the miraculous; and not once is an appeal made to it in Christ's later career. It is hardly credible that the vision of the shepherds on the night of the Nativity, and the visit of the wise men from the East, left no traces on the popular imagination. After all, thirty years is not a long period, and for a nation like the Jewish nation, the marvellous is remembered with infinite care and delight. No doubt the traditions survived; perhaps even they acquired volume and strength with time. But there is one providential circumstance told in the Gospels which alters the case completely: the rapid and prolonged

---

[1] St. John vii. 30.   [2] St. John viii. 20.
[3] St. John xii. 23.   [4] St John xiii. 1.

THE TRANSITION

change of abode of the family round which there had been the momentary glory. The disappearance into Egypt of the 'Holy Family,' told by St. Matthew (chapter ii.), deprived the glorious tale of its hero, and instead of making the reputation of Mary's Son, it helped to swell the volume of fair legends that made everybody look to the immediate coming of the Messiah. Far from helping Christ's cause, they went against Him, as the fact of His having been born at Bethlehem was not known. 'Of that multitude therefore, when they had heard these words of his, some said, This is the prophet indeed. Others said, This is the Christ. But some said, Doth the Christ come out of Galilee? Doth not the scripture say: that Christ cometh of the seed of David, and from Bethlehem, the town where David was? So there arose a dissension among the people because of him.'[1] If the memory of the vision of the shepherds and of the star had survived, the carpenter from Galilee was to be the very last person to be associated with it. There was no such interruption in the traditions round the person of John the Baptist. 'And fear came upon all their neighbours; and all these things were noised abroad over all the hill country of Judea. And all they that had heard them laid them up in their hearts, saying, What an one, think ye, shall this child be? For the hand of the

[1] St. John vii. 40-43.

Lord was with him.'[1] He was in the desert, it is true, but never far from the hills that had re-echoed the marvels of his birth. 'And the child grew, and was strengthened in spirit, and was in the deserts until the day of his manifestation to Israel.'[2] It is not surprising therefore to find that the moment he showed himself to the world, without any miracle or signs on his part, he should have been thought Christ by the most sincere of the Jews. 'And as the people were of opinion, and all were thinking in their hearts of John, that perhaps he might be the Christ; John answered, saying unto all, I indeed baptise you with water; but there shall come one mightier than I, the latchet of whose shoes I am not worthy to loose: he shall baptise you with the Holy Ghost and with fire.'[3] John's birth coincided closely enough with the period of the visit of the magi; nothing was easier than to associate him vaguely with the events of Christ's birth. It is certainly a surprising thing that this offspring of the tribe of Levi should have been hailed as the Christ with such readiness, when it was one of the staunchest beliefs of the Jewish people that Christ would be the son of David.

But if anything becomes clear, through the careful analysis of the New Testament documents,

[1] St. Luke i. 65, 66. [2] St. Luke i. 80.
[3] St. Luke iii. 15, 16.

THE TRANSITION

it is this: the Son of Mary was the very last man who would have had the benefit of the Messianic legends and hopes, so ripe in the Jewish nation of His day. He had to stand on the strength of His own divine powers. To say that Christ owed His success to a clever use and exploitation of the popular Messianic expectations of the day is an open contempt of written history.

CHAPTER XXII

CHRIST'S SINCERITY

CHRIST'S life is the greatest of all biographies. It contains the root-elements of every biography worth reading : intense sincerity pitted against the elementary human passions of jealousy, pride, avarice, and cowardice, and these elements are found in their highest human power.

It would be an immense spiritual loss to us if the thought of Christ's omnipotent control over His own destiny were apprehended by us in a sense that would diminish the sincerity and reality of the Christ-tragedy. We could never love deeply and perseveringly one in whose career there are unrealities, even if the unrealities were for the highest end. Thus if the treason of Judas had not been to Christ a disappointment as keen and as human as any betraying of confidence might be to me, the Lord's Passion would not be able to rivet my wondering sympathy.

But we easily fall a prey to our limited imagination, when our thoughts are busy with Christ.

We put the operations of His Godhead there, from where He had withdrawn them. The impression under which we constantly live, that after all Christ had it in His power to avoid all the evils that befell Him, sometimes paralyzes our attempts to penetrate more deeply into the wonderful human sequel of the great biography. Now, though it is the saint's constant wonderment that Christ, having it in His power to escape from his enemies, did not escape, such a consideration is conducive to a deeper love of Christ then only when it is coupled with the consideration that the exercise of such a power would have meant a redemption inferior to the redemption under which we live now. If Christ did not exert His power, it was because there were grave reasons for Him to act thus, and the reasons were connected with man's greater spiritual welfare.

The primary fact in Christ's history is His appearing in 'the form of a servant, being made in the likeness of men, and in habit found as a man.' It is the all-pervading element of the great biography, it is the one great fact which nothing could alter, because God had decided that for mankind's salvation such a form of incarnation was best. As great men are born with their characters, and as they are born into a definite state of human things, and as nothing can alter this primary fact, so likewise Christ had to appear in the form of a servant. No doubt it was in God's power to have made an incarnation that would not start with the form of a servant, but with the glory of the heir. But the former having been selected, for the higher spiritual exaltation of the human race, Christ's life was bound to be a tragedy.

This is why Our Lord's life may easily be studied according to the canons of ordinary human biography, and why it is found to be of all biographies the greatest. When I use the expression 'ordinary human biography,' I do not of course forget Christ's miraculous powers.

But taking for granted a miracle-working Christ, as you take for granted, say, a preternaturally far-sighted statesman, I say that, according to the canons of human biographies, a Christ who persisted in keeping hid within Himself His Godhead, out of charity for man, and who had to win faith in His Godhead by miracles, could easily become the world's greatest tragedy.

From the moment Christ makes His first public appearance up to the sealing of His sepulchre by public authorities, 'lest the disciples come and steal His body,' there is nothing that need surprise us; in fact, it does not surprise us. If once we have mastered the character of the Pharisee, we can foresee that there is little chance for Christ.

This is the reason why men of every school of

thought are able to make of the Gospels their life study. Even the rationalist, who does not believe in Christ's Divinity, is found to say true and illuminating things concerning the psychological sequel of Christ's human career. No one but a madman will deny that Christ stood amongst His contemporaries with a power and a majesty such as no man ever possessed. A little good will would be enough to identify Christ's superhuman position with Christ's power of miracles. But this superhuman attitude once accepted, the Gospels are a human biography. Christ's claim to be the Son of God explains the jealousy of the Pharisee, because Christ was to all appearances a man, and because He supported His claim with undoubted miracles. ' I and the Father are one. The Jews then took up stones to stone him. Jesus answered them, Many good works I have shewed you from my Father ; for which of those works do you stone me ? The Jews answered him, For a good work we stone thee not, but for blasphemy ; and because that thou, being a man, makest thyself God.' [1]

' The chief priests therefore and the Pharisees gathered a council, and said, What do we ? for this man doeth many miracles. If we let him alone so, all will believe in him ; and the Romans will come and take away our place and nation.' [2]

Nothing could express better the whole situation

[1] St. John x. 30-33.   [2] St. John xi. 47, 48.

than those words. The miracle-worker, being a man, claims oneness with the Father; let Him suffer the death of the blasphemer. His miracles are a danger.

The Pharisee, the man who sins against the Holy Ghost, ought to be our chief character-study in connection with the Gospels. If once we have fathomed him, we see easily that the Son of Mary is doomed to death, unless He depart from that great reserve that makes Him hide His Divinity. Judas, Pilate, Herod, the mocking soldiery, the scourging, the crowning with thorns, the crucifixion, become events that explain themselves naturally, through the ordinary elementary hatreds and weaknesses of human nature.

There are many passages in the New Testament pointing to the co-operation of Satan in bringing about Christ's death on the cross. It is a favourite theme with writers of all periods to make the drama of our Redemption reach the climax when Satan knows that he has destroyed his own kingdom, when he finds out that the Christ murdered at his suggestion was the Son of God, and that the death on the cross invented by satanic jealousy was God's preordained means of saving mankind.

We may easily grant such dramatic presentment of the Redemption without there being occasioned by it the least flaw in the human sequel of events in the Christ-biography. Satan's co-operation with man's act, far from superseding human activity or filling up gaps in the causal series of human events, depends entirely on human perverseness and wickedness for its own efficacy. The powers of darkness cannot work except in darkness, and the dark conscience of the Pharisees was more than ready to receive the suggestions of the spirit of wickedness in high places. Satan's share in the Crucifixion, far from rendering the Christ tragedy less human, gave it on the contrary an additional human cruelty and grimness, as Satan's work is always to stir up the deepest and darkest instincts of the corrupt human heart.

What we all ought to bear in mind is the human origin and the human sequel of the Christ-tragedy. Once it is granted that ' it behoved Him in all things to be made like unto His brethren, that He might become a merciful and faithful high priest before God,' [1]—once it is granted that the best Redemption was the most absolute identification of Christ with ordinary human conditions, there was enough love and enough hatred in man to bring about the Christ-tragedy. How in God's wisdom the prescience of it all could become the will of His heart does not belong to the created plane of thinking. On the one hand there is the clear fact of human sin, the greatest of all sins, the sin against the Holy Ghost, which is the full and direct human cause, and,

[1] Heb. ii. 17.

to all appearance, the total cause of Christ's death. On the other hand there is the fact of revelation that it was the Father's will that mankind should be saved by death on the cross.

No finite mind is able to grasp the harmonious interlocking of those two great causes: an infinitely holy will and an immensely perverted will. Infinitude of power and wisdom is the only explanation. 'The Father gave up Christ (to death) and He Himself gave Himself up out of charity, and therefore They are praised for it. But Judas gave Him up out of jealousy, Pilate gave Him up out of worldly fear because he feared Caesar, and therefore they are blamed."[1] No happier and shorter proposition could be framed to state the causalities at work in Christ's fate than this simple answer of St. Thomas to an objector who could not see how 'The Father' and Judas could both be said to have delivered up the Son of God.

In the same article St. Thomas thus defines the Father's rôle in Christ's Passion. 'God the Father delivered up Christ to suffering in a threefold way: Firstly, as far as He in His eternal will preordained Christ's passion to be the deliverance of the human race. Secondly, as far as He inspired Christ with the willingness to suffer for us, pouring Charity into Him. . . . Thirdly, not saving Him from suffering, but leaving Him at the mercy of His

[1] Quest. 47, art. 3.

persecutors.' Christ's own share in bringing on Himself the great storm is thus analysed by St. Thomas in the first article of the same question: ' One is the cause of an event indirectly, because one does not prevent it, when one could : just as a man is said to pour water on some one else, because he does not shut the window through which rain comes in. And it is in this wise that Christ Himself was the cause of His own suffering and death. For He could have prevented His suffering and death, firstly checking His enemies, so as to render them incapable or unwilling to kill Him. Secondly, because His spirit had power to preserve intact the nature of His body, lest it should succumb under any lesion, which power Christ's soul possessed because it was united with the Word of God in oneness of person. Therefore as the soul of Christ did not keep from the body the hurts inflicted on it, but rather as it willed that the bodily nature should succumb under the infliction, Christ is said to have given up His life, or to have died willingly.'

But such power, again, Christ could not have exerted without our Redemption being less bountiful, and if He was to give Himself to man without reserve or restriction, He had to be the helpless prey of man's darkest passions. The Father would have sent Him twelve legions of angels, if He had asked, in virtue of His birthright. But how could one with twelve legions of angels surrounding Him turn round and look at Peter with a look that brought the truest and warmest tears to human eyes that were ever shed? 'And Peter, going out, wept bitterly. And the men that held Him mocked him, and struck him, and they blindfolded him, and smote his face.'[1] It is from the midst of such a gathering of lowest humanity that Christ won back the faithless disciple to a penitent love that was to be stronger than death.

[1] St. Luke xxii. 62-64.

CHAPTER XXIII

THE GREAT LIFE

CHRIST'S mortal career is a most complete and most perfect act in itself; it has a fulness that makes it a source of life for all ages to come.

It is perhaps not too much to say that the general tendency of the human mind is a tendency to belittle the importance of the individual life—I mean the mortal career of individual people. Man soon begins to dream of possible new existences for the same individual where things might be done and duties might be fulfilled which have been omitted and neglected during the first mortal life. One need only remember the doctrine of the migration of souls, the most wide-spread theory on the Hereafter we know of; no doubt, as most human lives look so worthless, man's innate wish for better things makes such beliefs part of the human optimism.

Christianity is indeed of all religions the most optimistic religion; but its optimism never degenerates into a vagueness of hope; its optimism is essentially this, that it thinks highly of the possibilities of the one mortal life of which we are certain as being the one chance for every individual. Christianity constantly reins in the human imagination, only too prone to overlook the blessings of the present hour for the fairy tales of uncertain existences in the future.

Christ's mortal life has become to Christ's Church the beginning and the end, the Alpha and the Omega, the consummation of all sanctity, the source of all grace. There is no re-acting of that great life; it has been acted once, and the act was indeed a delight to the eyes of God and of the Angels of God.

Christ Himself insists emphatically on the importance of His one life, to do the work of His Father. 'And Jesus passing by saw a man who was blind from his birth. And his disciples asked him: Rabbi, who hath sinned, this man, or his parents, that he should be born blind? Jesus answered, Neither hath this man sinned, nor his parents; but that the works of God should be made manifest in him. I must work the works of him that sent me, whilst it is day: the night cometh, when no man can work. As long as I am in the world, I am the light of the world.'[1]

'I have glorified thee on the earth: I have finished the work which thou gavest me to do. And now glorify thou me, O Father, with thyself, with the glory which I had, before the world was, with thee.'[2]

[1] St. John ix. 1-5. [2] St. John xvii. 4, 5.

This same theological idea is one of the leading thoughts in that most perfect *résumé* of Christology : the Epistle to the Hebrews. ' Then said I, Behold I come to do thy will, O God. He taketh away the first, that he may establish that which followeth. In the which will we are sanctified by the oblation of the body of Jesus Christ once. And every priest indeed standeth daily ministering, and often offering the same sacrifices, which can never take away sins. But this man, offering one sacrifice for sins, for ever sitteth on the right hand of God ; from henceforth expecting until his enemies be made his footstool. For by one oblation he hath perfected for ever them that are sanctified. And the Holy Ghost also doth testify this to us ; for after that he said, And this is the testament which I will make unto them after those days, saith the Lord. I will give my laws in their hearts, and on their minds will I write them : And their sins and iniquities I will remember no more. Now where there is a remission of these, there is no more an oblation for sin.' [1]

In another chapter I shall show how this oneness of life in Christ is not contradicted but rather emphasised by the doctrine of the Christian Eucharist ; but there is one remark I should like to make here. It is the impression of the writer of this book that certain pious folks have not been proof against that weakness of the human mind mentioned

[1] Heb. x. 9-18.

above, the tendency of multiplying lives, because the first life somehow seems to lack fulness and sufficiency. Not a small amount of modern eucharistic literature is tainted with this tendency. Good men and pious men make of the Eucharistic Presence a kind of second existence of Christ, a kind of mortal career that goes on for ever and ever, a kind of self-abasement on the part of the Son of God greater even than His first abasement.

Now, I should be the very last person to put a check on the enthusiasm of Christian feeling round the great sacramental marvel. With St. Thomas Aquinas I say here:

Quantum potes, tantum aude ;	All words of thine but feebly tell
Quia major omni laude,	Thy God's transcendent worth ;
Nec laudare sufficis.	Yet let thy loud rejoicings swell
	And reach the ends of earth.
	Missal. Sequence.

At the same time there is the great fact that Christ's mortal career was all fulness, and that through His resurrection He entered into glory for ever.

The presence and existence of Christ in the Holy Eucharist are not a human presence, a human existence, in the sense in which He was present or existent in His mortal days. It is not even a presence or existence that resembles in any way Christ's glorified presence and existence in heaven, such as He is now. It is a presence, it is an existence which is absolutely new, infinitely different from any known mode of presence and existence.

People who talk of the Eucharistic Presence in language that could not apply to anything except an ordinary human life could do nothing better than study the seventy-sixth question of the third part of the Summa, with its eight highly metaphysical articles. 'The manner according to which Christ is in this Sacrament.' But let me quote from the seventh article, whether Christ's body, such as it is in this sacrament, could be seen by a bodily eye, at least if the bodily eye were that of a glorified (risen) body. 'Therefore, speaking quite accurately, Christ's body, according to the manner of existence which It has in this sacrament, is not discernible either by sense or imagination, but by the intellect only, which is called the spiritual eye. It is however perceived differently, according to the differences of intellect. For as the mode of existence, according to which Christ is in this sacrament, is entirely supernatural, it can be seen in its proper state by the supernatural intellect—I mean the divine intellect; and as a consequence it can be seen by the glorified intellect of either angel or man, who through the vision of the divine essence, in virtue of that participated clarity of the divine intellect in them, see things that are supernatural. As for the intellect of man still in his mortal career, it cannot see it except by faith, as is the case with all things supernatural. But even the angelic intellect, left to its natural resources, is unable to see Christ's (sacramental) body. Therefore the demons cannot see through their intellect Christ in this sacrament, except by faith.'

Church history is full of marvellous events centring round the consecrated elements of the Eucharist, such as palpable flesh taking the place of the consecrated Host, or warm blood issuing forth from the sacramental Element, or even the Eucharistic Bread taking the form of the Divine Infant, for the consolation of the faithful or the conviction of the doubter. St. Thomas treats of the objective value of such miraculous phenomena in the eighth article of the same question lxxvi. His explanations are satisfying; the phenomenon is either a subjective impression in the beholder, or an objective preternatural and permanent effect round about the consecrated species. But the real substance of Christ's body does not come into the phenomenon; it remains hid in its inaccessible mysteriousness. 'Such transformed sacramental elements,' he says, ' have sometimes been shut up and reserved, at the suggestion of a body of bishops, in a pyx. *Quod nefas esset de Christo sentire secundum propriam speciem.* It would be wickedness to hold such opinion of Christ in His proper nature.'

This energetic condemnation on the part of Aquinas of the idea of Christ being shut up, a prisoner as it were, in material surroundings, though it be under a eucharistic transformation, shows well how repugnant to Catholic theology are ways of stating the Eucharist Presence in other terms than those of the sacramental Transubstantiation.

There are two distinct points of doctrine with regard to the great Christian Eucharist. The first point is the Real Presence : Christ is really present. This is the point over which Christians are divided, some being satisfied with a mystical, spiritual presence of Christ's body, whilst others, taking the Gospel literally, hold that besides the mystical spiritual presence, Christ's bodily reality is there, and that the spiritual, the mystical reality is an effect, an outflow of the bodily reality thus present. This first point contains nothing as to the manner of that bodily presence.

The second point is an exclusively Catholic point ; it has long been part of the Catholic theology on the blessed Eucharist, and the Council of Trent raised it to a Catholic dogma. It is the dogma of Transubstantiation, the dogma, I might say, of the mode of Christ's presence. Christ is there, in the consecrated element, because the consecrated element has been changed, transubstantiated into Christ's body, by God's omnipotence, not by a kind of 'impanation,' of taking up His abode in the bread, as Lutheran theology would have it. It is easy to see how the Catholic doctrine of Transubstantiation removes the mode of Christ's Eucharistic Presence into the region of the mysterious and miraculous beyond any other theory. A Catholic ought to be the very last man to apply to Christ's Eucharistic Presence modes of speech that sound ludicrous when not applied to the normal, natural human life, with its lights and its shadows, its trials and its virtues.

I have risked wearying the reader with the refutation of possible aberrations of Catholic piety, because I feel how important it is for our spiritual life to go back constantly to Christ's mortal life, to find there not only every virtue and every example, but also finality of virtue and of example.

'Who in the days of his flesh, with a strong cry and tears, offering up prayers and supplications to him that was able to save him from death, was heard for his reverence. And whereas he indeed was the Son of God, he learned obedience by the things which he suffered; and being consummated he became, to all that obey him, the cause of eternal salvation.' [1]

In another chapter I shall show the relation-

[1] Heb. v. 7, 8, 9.

ship between the Eucharist and Christ's life and death. But whatever that relationship, Christ, like all other *viatores*, pilgrims on earth, has only one earthly life, one human life, one life of prayer, and struggle, and merit, and edification, for His brethren : the life of thirty-three years in Palestine. Everything in the spiritual order, not excepting the Eucharist itself, comes from that great life, and goes back to it. Christ's Eucharistic Presence cannot be called a human life ; it cannot be said to show forth human virtues ; it cannot be regarded as containing ethical perfections that might be a pattern to the Christian, or ethical perfections in any way superior to the ethical perfections of His mortal career. It is a presence so eminently miraculous, so absolutely beyond the laws of humanity, that God alone is able to watch the pulsation of that hidden life.

In order to remain faithful to my programme of describing the Christ of theology, I have to confine myself to one aspect of the great life, the theological aspect. We are happily in possession of excellent works, endless in their variety, on the historical and spiritual aspects of the great life. Now the aspect of the great life, which, to my mind, constitutes something deeply interesting for the religious thinker, is the circumstance that Christ led an ordinary social life, with the duties appropriate to refined and civilised humanity.

He differs from the Baptist ; He is not a solitary, an ascetic, a priest of the Levitical tribe ; He is the son of David, of the tribe of Juda, of royal descent. ' For he of whom these things are spoken is of another tribe, of which no one attended the altar. For it is evident that our Lord sprang out of Juda ; in which tribe Moses spoke nothing concerning priests.' [1]

This ordinariness of Christ's life is a fact of such significance that I do not hesitate to call it its theological aspect, because it is an immense acquisition to the history of human sanctity and human spiritualness that the Son of God on earth should have led a life not different in its external arrangements from the ordinary social life of the men of His time and His social standing. ' Is not this the carpenter, the Son of Mary ? ' [2] This exclamation on the lips of Christ's nearest acquaintances shows well how completely human He had made Himself, and how unprepared the Jewish mind was to receive its heaven from the hands of an artisan whom they had met daily for years past.

Nothing could be more suggestive, from the point of view of the history of religion, than the differences between the career of the Baptist and the career of Christ. The Baptist was essentially and deeply a Jewish saint from beginning to end. Christ was not the kind of saint the Jew admired

---

[1] Heb. vii. 13, 14.   [2] St. Mark vi. 3.

or could understand. John the Baptist was never contradicted, he was never doubted by the people, his mode of life was such as to make every word that fell from his lips a rule of faith. The Pharisee might indeed say of John, ' He hath a devil.' [1] But then John had never spared them. ' Ye brood of vipers, who hath shewed you to flee from the wrath to come ? ' [2] Such had been the Baptist's apostrophe to them. As for the people themselves, their faith in John was implicit. ' And it came to pass, that on one of the days, as he was teaching the people in the temple, and preaching the gospel, the chief priests and the scribes, with the ancients, met together and spoke to him, saying : Tell us by what authority dost thou these things ? Who is he that hath given thee this authority ? And Jesus answering said to them, I will also ask you one thing. Answer me : The baptism of John, was it from heaven, or of men ? But they thought within themselves, saying : If we shall say, From heaven, he will say ; Why then did you not believe him ? But if we say, Of men ; the whole people will stone us : for they are persuaded that John was a prophet. And they answered that they knew not whence it was. And Jesus said to them, Neither do I tell you by what authority I do these things.' [3]

That one of so perfect a life should give testimony to one whose mode of conversing in the world was

[1] St. Matt. xi. 18.   [2] St. Matt. iii. 7.   [3] St. Luke xx. 1-8.

like any other man's conversing was indeed a great puzzle to Christ's contemporaries. Christ was at an enormous disadvantage with the Jewish mind, owing to this ordinariness of life. His miracles, his wonderful teaching, were no compensation to the Jewish temperament for that absence of ascetical austerity. It was rather a scandal unto them that one with an ordinary kind of life should do wonders and speak such wisdom. Had he been amongst them, 'not eating and drinking,' the miracles would have been hailed with enthusiasm. 'And going out from thence, he went into his own country; and his disciples followed him. And when the sabbath was come, he began to teach in the synagogue: and many hearing him were in admiration of his doctrine, saying, How came this man by all these things? And what wisdom is this that is given to him, and such mighty works as are wrought by his hands? Is not this the carpenter, the son of Mary, the brother of James, and Joseph, and Jude, and Simon? Are not also his sisters here with us? And they were scandalised in regard of him.'[1] 'And they come to a house, and the multitude cometh together again, so that they could not so much as eat bread. And when his friends had heard of it, they went out to lay hold on him; for they said, He is become mad.'[2]

That spiritual greatness was possible within the

[1] St. Mark vi. 1-3.   [2] St. Mark iii. 19, 20, 21.

ordinary conditions of human society was a truth not yet realised. That a man could sit down to dinner with his host and read at the same time the secrets of the heart of those that approached him was a lesson still to be learned by men. Jesus had multiplied signs and wonders, but He failed to win the confidence of the Jews. John had done no sign, and yet his word was of immense weight. ' If I do not the works of my Father, believe me not. But if I do, though you will not believe me, believe the works : that you may know, and believe, that the Father is in me, and I in the Father. They sought therefore to take him : and he escaped out of their hands. And he went again beyond the Jordan, into that place where John was baptising first ; and there he abode. And many resorted to him, and they said, John indeed did no sign. But all things, whatsoever John said of this man were true. And many believed in him.' [1]

St. Thomas treats of the characteristics of Christ's life in the fortieth question of the third part of the Summa. *De modo conversationis Christi* is the title of the treatise. I quote from the commentary of Cajetan on the second article, as embodying in a few words the essence of Christian theology as to Christ's practical life amongst men. ' Take notice and fix in your mind this doctrine, viz. that Christ was an example of perfection in all

[1] St. John x. 37-42.

things that belong necessarily to salvation. From this you conclude that in those things which have no necessary relation to salvation, things that have no intrinsic goodness, but are good merely as means to an end, such as obedience, poverty, and other such practices, we ought not to ask from Christ more austere things, as if they were more perfect. But what we ought to find in Christ are the things that belong to the final purpose of the Incarnation; whether such things be austere practices or not, matters little.'

The great life is indeed an infinitely wise life, because all its phases and all its duties are determined by this one consideration. It was a wisdom of life the Jew could not understand; for him a garment of camel's hair was the spiritual marvel. It is only the children of wisdom that can see the beauty of that other life. ' The Son of man is come eating and drinking; and you say, Behold a man that is a glutton and a drinker of wine, a friend of publicans and sinners! And wisdom is justified by all her children.' [1]

I may once more quote Cajetan, summing up the doctrine of his great master, St. Thomas. The terseness of the theologian is very helpful, as it is so important for us all to take a true and sober view of Christ's glorious life, the divinely authentic pattern of human perfection. ' Christ adopted quite

[1] St. Luke vii. 34, 35.

appropriately social life as His mode of conversing on earth, not solitary life. Such is the thesis of St. Thomas. Now this is thus proven. Christ was bound to adopt such a mode of life as would best suit the purpose of the Incarnation. The purpose of the Incarnation is best served by social life. Therefore Christ was bound to choose social life as His life. The purpose of the Incarnation is threefold : first, to give testimony of the truth ; second, to save sinners ; third, to bring men to God. Now, all this means social life.'[1]

[1] Commentary on first article of the fortieth question.

CHAPTER XXIV

GOD MEETING GOD

PERSONALITY, in the sense of its being a great entitative reality, is, as I have said so often, at the root of all the metaphysical momentum of Hypostatic Union.

Personality, in the sense of its being a living, overpowering influence, is at the root of all our sanctification and exaltation in Christ. The two views are not separable in practice, as Christ is a Divine Person through that wondrous replacement of personality so much spoken of in this book, for our sakes, in order that we should gain highest human perfection in Him.

Personality, in so far as it signifies a rational being with distinct rights and claims, with a distinct ethical estate as its inalienable property, is at the root of that part of Christology called Christ's Priesthood. This third view of personality is not separable from the two preceding views, in practice. But it is the predominating view when we come to approach Christ's atonement—Christ's sacerdotal rôle.

Theologians have written whole folio-volumes on this single question: 'The Priesthood of Christ.' It seems no easy task to compress so great a thesis into one single chapter. However, I have the example of St. Thomas Aquinas, who finds that one *quaestio* (the twenty-sixth), with six articles, is sufficient even for the theologian. Besides, there is the inspired treatise on Christ's Priesthood, the Epistle to the Hebrews, a strictly theological thesis with Rabbinic argumentation pressed effectively into service.

The question might be asked whether Christ's priestly office is anything different from His other offices; for instance, from His office as the mystical Head of the Church. My answer is that the distinction is not clearly drawn anywhere, either in the Apostolic writings or even in the theology of St. Thomas. Atonement, mediation, sanctification, teaching, consoling, are all functions that may be attributed to priesthood. The definition of a priest, given in the Epistle to the Hebrews, covers all such beneficent interventions on the part of the God-man. 'For every high priest taken from among men is ordained for men in the things that appertain to God, that he may offer up gifts and sacrifices for sins: who can have compassion on them that are ignorant and that err; because he himself also is compassed with infirmity.'[1] Christ

[1] Heb. v. 1, 2.

is an entirely supernatural personage; Him 'the Father hath sanctified and sent into the world.'[1] He is the great Anointed of God; His whole bearing, His whole presence is that of a high priest; He is a priest always and everywhere.

There is, however, the essential, the untransferable act of priesthood, that of offering a sacrifice; and it is with that function of Christ I am concerned now, as in it we find the greatest assertion of the mystery of His Personality, what I might be pardoned for calling the juridical assertion.

By the replacement of human personality in Christ through Divine Personality, He is a Divine Person with a power for created life and created virtue, which life and virtue have infinite ethical value, as they are attributable to a Divine Person, and as a Divine Person is responsible for them. Christ is a Divine Person, with a distinct Personality from that of the Father.

Christ exerted highest virtue, highest love, in the death on the cross, and He gave glory to God through His obedience, coupled with equality of personal rights with the Father.

Theologians have gone deep into the juridical question of the Atonement; their labours, though very arduous, make one point quite clear: Christian atonement differs, *toto coelo*, from the instinct of atonement which is practically the common inherit-

[1] St. John x. 36.

GOD MEETING GOD

ance of mankind. It is not the physical death, the physical blood, that is the primary thing in the Christian atonement; it is the great personal factor of God treating with God. According to Christian theology, far from there being 'a wantonness of blood,' there is in the sacrifice of Christ a divine nicety as to the measure of the immolation.

The Atonement is a moral claim, according to theologians, meaning by the word moral ' juridical.' No Christian can exclude from his theology such thoughts on the Redemption as are based on the juridical claims of a Divine Person.

The difference of the Christian atonement from the human atonements—the Jewish not excluded—is beautifully put forward in the Epistle to the Hebrews, where the personal value as opposed to the merely physical value is so strongly emphasised.

' For it is impossible that with the blood of oxen and goats sin should be taken away. Wherefore when he cometh into the world, he saith : Sacrifice and oblation thou wouldest not, but a body thou hast fitted to me : holocausts for sin did not please thee. Then said I, Behold, I come : in the head of the book it is written of me that I should do thy will, O God. In saying before, Sacrifices and oblations and holocausts for sin thou wouldest not, neither are they pleasing to thee, which are offered according to the law. Then said I : Behold, I come to do thy will, O God. He taketh away the first, that he may establish that which followeth. In the which will we are sanctified by the oblation of the body of Jesus Christ once.'[1]

There is a further consideration indispensable in this matter of Christ's Atonement : it is the additional sanctity acquired by Christ through the obedience of the cross. His original sanctity that manifested itself in His wonderful life was not to be the price of our Redemption. There had been no juridical transaction between Divine Persons as to its moral purchasing power. The Passion, on the contrary, was made the price of our souls. The following passage of St. Thomas is very illuminating. ' The original sanctity of Christ's humanity does not prevent that same human nature when it is offered up to God in the Passion from being sanctified in a new way—that is to say, as a victim actually offered up. It then acquired from its original charity and from that grace of (Hypostatic) Union that sanctifies it, absolutely speaking, the actual sanctification of victim.'[2]

[1] Heb. x. 4-10   [2] Question 22, art. 2, ad. 3 um.

CHAPTER XXV

THE MAN OF SORROWS

THE incomprehensible refinement of a Divine Personality is not only the most enduring motive for Christian compunction over the crucified Saviour, it is also the explanation of the greatest of Christ's sufferings. None of us can fail to be deeply affected by the story of the Passion, if our minds are busy habitually with the infinitely sweet excellencies of the Son of God made man. Compassion for Christ crucified will remain an actual living thing in human souls as long as the world lasts, chiefly because the Sufferer was an infinitely excellent person. Compassion enduring to the end of time is not a fruitless or groundless wail, in such a case.

But, as I said, Christ's personal perfections of being were also the measure of His sufferings, both in soul and mind.

It is a general Christian conviction that Christ in Himself suffered more than any other human creature on earth. St. Thomas adopts this view in his question forty-six.[1]

I must confess to a certain anger with inferior spiritual literature that seems to enjoy a horror like a feast, and which has a mania for an accumulation of horrors, if once let loose. Such men, for instance, would speak of ten thousand years of purgatory with as much ease as of one year. Once satisfied that they may use the figures, they make it centuries or seconds with the same generosity. It is a type of a raw religious mind, good in itself, but hopelessly callous to the rights of reason.

So in this matter of Christ's sufferings, one has read books written by devout men in which the accumulation of pain in Christ's life has been done with a kind of mad recklessness, with utter disregard of the Gospel narrative and of theological principles. In fact, such accumulation, bad as the taste is, defeats its own end : it takes Christ's Passion out of the human sphere, and makes it profitless to us as an example and as a consolation.

The thesis of St. Thomas, however, that Christ suffered more than any other single man ever did, is common Christian sentiment, and it is wonderfully helpful in the struggle of life.

'From all these causes,' says St. Thomas at the end of the article I have quoted, 'it is clear

[1] Quest. 46, art. 6.

THE MAN OF SORROWS 183

that the pain of Christ was the greatest of all pains.'

It would be difficult to assign any single cause that gives to Christ's sufferings such proportions: there are many causes at work, coming from the complexity of His wonderful Personality.

His physical torments would go a long way to make of Him one of the most ill-treated human beings, chiefly if they are taken in connection with the ingratitudes and the treasons that brought them about. But when all has been said, in order to give the explanation how Christ's suffering was simply and absolutely 'the greatest,' we have to fall back on the perfection of His hypostatically united nature. Christ's body was a miracle of perfection and delicacy. His soul was the finest instrument of feeling that ever was. On a body of such complexion, tortures like those described so soberly in the Gospel narratives would assume unwonted proportions, which sufferings no special heavenly consolations seem to have sweetened, when the pain was actually on Him. In His mind, He voluntarily admitted sorrow for sin, for failure in the spiritual world, and His keen soul became its own tormentor. In this matter of Christ's spiritual sufferings over the sins of the world there seems to be no knowable limits. How much did He allow Himself to be invaded by that keen internal sorrow? 'Christ,' says St. Thomas, ' in order to satisfy for the sins of all men, took on Himself sadness, a sadness that was the greatest human sadness, as an absolute measure, but a sadness that did not go beyond the rule of sound reason.'[1]

St. Thomas makes another golden remark in connection with Christ's death. ' The bodily Life of Christ was of such excellency, and this chiefly on account of Divinity united (hypostatically), that loss even for an hour would be a matter of much greater sorrow than the loss of the life of any other man for any length of time.'[2]

The Passion of Christ ought to be a subject of tender thought, even for the most exact and most unemotional mind. There is not in it physical pain merely for the sake of a raw contempt of physical well-being. We know that it is voluntary in the sense of its not having been the only possible device God had to redeem the world, yet that there is in it a divine adaptation of most excellent means to a most excellent end is made manifest by the very choice God made of it to be the cause of our Redemption.

[1] Ad 2 um.   [2] Ad 4 um.

CHAPTER XXVI

THE HAPPINESS OF CHRIST

It would be a most ungracious and unnatural theology to speak of Christ's sorrows without even mentioning Christ's joys. The contemplation of Christ as the man of sorrow, if it were too exclusive, would become a positive heresy, as such exclusiveness would mean that Christ was the great sufferer by a kind of wild fatality, that He was the personification of the *Weltschmerz*, of the world's unspoken agony.

With all our faith in Christ's vicarious atonement; with all the literalness of inspired language, such as St. Paul's expression,[1] ' Him that knew no sin, for us he hath made sin'; with all the bitterness of Christ's death,—the theological fact remains, that the element of joy in Christ's human life was immensely preponderant.

We must bear in mind that there was never in Christ any struggling after happiness, or even after higher happiness, out of unhappiness. He con-

[1] 2 Cor. v. 21.

descended to put aside, partially, happiness for a time ; but there is never in Him the grim stretching forward to life and light that characterises the earthly hero. His mortality and passibility were temporary arrangements of a miraculous nature, and though the cessation of such an arrangement was to be in a sense Christ's human reward, it differed profoundly from our release from this body of sin, inasmuch as we are released from a fatal and universal law, whilst Christ's glorification was the cessation of the miraculous suspension of glorification. When Christ entered into that personal glory that was His birthright, He entered into it in a spirit of triumph, with ' greater honour,' as St. Thomas says in article six of the forty-ninth question. But being the heir, not a stranger, it was merely 'a home-coming' when He received the totality of His happiness.

The Christ of the Gospels is as much the source of life and joy to the millions of human souls that worship Him as is the Christ of Heaven. He could be no such support if His mortal existence had been unalloyed agony.

The doctrine of St. Thomas as to the fulness and the perseverance of Christ's bliss is most constant and most unequivocal. Christ had beatific vision from the first moment of His conception in Mary's womb. His beatific vision was immensely greater than the visions of all other created spirits put together. His soul had the exceptional favour of being created in beatific vision, a state of blessedness not conferred on any other created mind.

I quote the third objection of the fourth article of the thirty-fourth question with its answer; it gives us in a few words the key to the mystery of Christ's exceptional position in the scale of happiness. The objection is as follows : ' What belongs neither to man, nor to the angel, seems to be the attribute of God Himself ; and therefore it cannot belong to Christ, as far as He is man. But always to be happy (through beatific vision) belongs neither to man nor to the angel ; for if they had been created happy (through beatific vision) they would not have sinned afterwards. Therefore Christ as man was not happy (through beatific vision) from the first moment of His conception.'

The answer is short : ' I answer the third objection and say that Christ from the fact of His being God and man had even in His manhood something more excellent than other creatures—namely, that He should be happy (through beatific vision) from the very beginning.'

Far from making ' happiness ' for Himself the goal of a vehement struggle with the powers of sadness, the Christ of our theology holds an unprecedented position of bliss by His very birthright.

What beatific vision means as a source of

happiness is, of course, incomprehensible. Now, though it be part of the theology of St. Thomas that Christ put limits to certain of the secondary effects of that overpowering bliss, it would imply contradiction to say that He did not enjoy to the full the blessed vision itself. He was absolutely *beatus* in that portion of His mind where there was the vision. Again it would be contradictory to say that Christ's vision was ever interrupted. One might as well think of an interruption of Hypostatic Union itself. Such interruption, far from being helpful towards man's redemption, would have lessened its power, as it would have lessened Christ's natural dignity and sanctity. Another consideration that finds its place here is this : Beatific vision can never be anything but a source of happiness. All things seen in God are seen in their divine relationship, and as such they are good, and very good. Even the sight of a sinful world, as it can be seen in God's omniscience, could never be a sad spectacle—or, anyhow, a saddening spectacle—because the blessed vision shows that if a divine ordinance be transgressed by a creature in one way, another ordinance redresses the transgression. Christ could never be saddened from what He saw in the glory of the Father. But He had inferior orders of knowledge, and according to these His soul was made sad.

Many other joys there were in Christ's human

life besides that sun of brightness high up in His mind, the vision of God. How could a life of consummate virtuousness and sanctity be anything but a long spiritual feast?

But the greatest of merely human joys was, no doubt, His own immaculate Mother, in whose company almost the whole of His mortal life was spent. It is certainly a great light in itself, in matters of Christ's Personality, to reflect that He who came to save sinners spent His life, a few years excepted, with one who was pre-eminently not a sinner. It all points to the same great theological fact, that with Christ the law of happiness is the dominant, the prevailing law, the law that is followed up as far as possible. The law of suffering is submitted to as an exception, and with a wise adaptation of means to an end, whilst the law of happiness is applied with divine generosity.

CHAPTER XXVII

CHRIST THE STRONG ONE

THE duality of natures in Christ, being so much made of by our theology, has many interesting consequences. There is in Christ duality of saintship, duality of spiritualness; there is in Him a created and an increated sanctity; and, more than all that, there is in Him the saintship which is His own personal acquisition. Though He be the Son of God, sharing with God the privilege of matchless sanctity, He created Himself a sanctity of His own. He acquired sanctity, just as the son of an ancient family of inexhaustible patrimony might build up to himself a great fortune by personal initiative and activity, though he be the heir and lord of an ancient domain. 'And whereas indeed He was the Son of God, He learned obedience by the things which he suffered; and being consummated, He became to all that obey Him the cause of eternal salvation.'[1]

Christ practised human saintship in a heroic degree. He was full of sanctity, He was infinitely

[1] Heb. v. 8, 9.

remote from sin through the very elements of His wonderful Personality; yet human sanctity had for Him all the terrors high sanctity always brings with itself. Infinitely holy from the beginning, He had to be holy in a human way by mixing with ordinary humanity, and His native infinitude of purity made the struggle all the more tragical because opposition and sin, as well as physical suffering, became to Him more unbearable by reason of His own wonderful perfection of origin. It was divine sanctity endowed with the power of human sentiment, or, if we like, it was human sentiment made more keen through the presence of the infinite Purity.

There is nothing so tragical, nothing so remote from unreality and shallowness as the life of a man of superior intelligence and high resolve bent on doing some great work for the men that surround him, and with the concurrence of those that are to be ultimately benefited, but being misunderstood, misjudged, distrusted all the time by those very men. Of all the tragedies it is the most bitter.

Such was Christ's saintship; in Him we find that bitter tragedy on an almost infinite scale. His native sanctity is like a fire devouring His soul; it is His zeal for the sanctification of man. 'And for them do I sanctify myself, that they also may be sanctified in truth.'[1]

[1] St. John xvii. 19.

Human resistance, human blindness, nay, even human sin against the Holy Ghost, are to Him the occasion of acquiring personal sanctity. Catholic theology therefore understood Christ better when it endowed Him from the very origin with every species of spiritual gift, because the human patience of Christ is so great, precisely because with so much native dignity of spirit Christ descended into the difficulties of human companionship.

There is in Our Lord's life an element of interest that is necessarily absent : it is the internal struggle between good and evil, the sifting of motives, the growth of wisdom through failures of selfish motives and untimely efforts. In other words, the element of passion in the ordinary sense of the word is entirely excluded from Our Lord's character. There might be the danger, therefore, that His life should appeal to us less as a living fact than as an abstract ideal. Yet Christ's life ought to be our constant solace, precisely because it was so intensely human and so intensely heroic in its human virtues.

We cannot of course think for one moment of moral struggle in connection with Our Lord's Personality. He never felt any dissensions in his mind or body. But there is in Our Lord's nature an element that made of His life the greatest struggle, the greatest tragedy. It was that contradiction between His own personal sanctity and his external surroundings.

He was indeed the Son of God come down from heaven, to live amongst short-sighted, prejudiced, ignorant, and sinful men; and he came to share, so to speak, their social position. There was the great struggle between this incomparable superiority and human inferiority. For, the moment He enters into the world, He identifies Himself with the men that surround Him.

He is not as one living amongst men and yet picking his steps carefully, raising his garment lest it be soiled, and saying to all that are near, 'Do not touch me, because I am clean.' No; He walks bravely with the sinner and the traitor, with the coward and the fanatic, for they are truly His friends. Their friendship and their good will have become indispensable to Him, if His work is to have roots in the human race. This intimate contact between Him and the living man was a necessary element in the Redemption. How could man be sanctified unless his heart had been won by God? Our Lord had to enter into the lives of His followers; He had to admit them into the hiddenness of His own life. It is in this contact between highest sanctity and human commonness that we are to find that element of conflict which lends to His life its human interest.

It is no doubt a spectacle for angels to see a being of clay, such as man is, rise gradually to the spiritual plane, through a series of disappointments in the things he had set his heart upon. But what shall we say of consummate sanctity and highest spiritualness giving itself to man as a friend, to be treated by him as a friend, in his own gross way of understanding and treating sanctity and spiritualness? For we shall see how the Son of God treats with man on the footing of equality; how He never uses His omnipotence to precipitate a conclusion, to overpower a mind with the impression of His own excellency. He is determined to let Himself be found by man, as no doubt any other way of convincing man would not be so deep, not so lasting.

The great truths of sacred theology concerning the God Incarnate are considered sometimes to be mere abstractions, incapable of giving life and colour to our Lord's Personality. Nothing could be less true. They all enter into the very life of Our Lord; they make that life one of palpitating interest, precisely because they give us the key to that incomparable superiority of Our Lord's nature, which superiority is of all things the one element we must constantly bear in mind if we are to understand Our Lord's life.

It is strange how an act or a word coming from a human being of some excellency sanctifies for ever the spot where the act was performed or the word was pronounced. We travel a thousand miles. and the country we go through is nothing to us.

We come to the spot where a human mind, a human heart have been at their best, were it only for a moment, and there we get easily lost in thought, so great is the impression.

Our Lord's excellency was such as to give to the very stones over which His shadow fell the power of melting the heart of the pure and simple.

CHAPTER XXVIII

THE MISUNDERSTANDINGS OF THE GOSPEL

IT is the law of all real greatness not to be understood. The great are great because they are above their surroundings, because they see farther or even differently. In every greatness there is a practical disregard of established ways and axioms. In our Lord's life there is this trait of greatness.

He is misunderstood, and His own did not understand Him. There are few things that are more pathetic than the conversation which St. Peter had with his Master shortly after Simon Peter had been promised the keys of the Kingdom of Heaven. 'It is then,' says the Evangelist, 'that Christ began to speak to them of what was going to happen; that He was going up to Jerusalem, there to be reviled by the high priests and the scribes, and to be put to death, and to rise on the third day. Then Simon Peter took Him aside and rebuked Him, saying, "Far be such things from thee."'

We can easily imagine St. Peter, strong in the conviction that he had his Master's confidence, and that therefore he could do what no one else could do, administer to him a gentle rebuke; he walks away with Him, and no doubt after a very polite introduction comes to the matter that weighs on his mind. He has a right to look after his Master's interests, and certainly he understands them as well as the Master Himself. The Master listens silently, and when Simon Peter has finished delivering himself of his carefully prepared rebuke, Christ turns round and looks on poor Peter with unusual sternness. The two had been walking side by side whilst Peter was unfolding his views. 'Take thyself behind me, thou Satan; for thou art a scandal unto me: thou savourest the things of man, not the things of God.' Peter was far from understanding his Master; with all his good will and his good intentions, and with all his loyalty to his Master, his mind was still moving on the plane of man. Our Lord's admonitions that follow directly after look very much like an answer to the remarks Peter must have made in his effort to dissuade the Master. 'If one wants to walk after me, let him take up his cross and follow me.' 'He that loseth his soul shall find it; and what does it profit a man if he gain the whole universe and suffer the loss of his soul?' 'For what shall man give for his soul? For the Son of man will come in the glory of his Father with the angels, and then he shall give to everyone according to his deserts. Amen, I say unto you, There are some standing here who will not die without having seen the Son of man in his glory.'

This last allusion to the Transfiguration, which was to take place a few days after, and in which Peter was to hold such a conspicuous place, seemed to be a kind of revulsion in our Lord's feeling towards Peter, after the sharp rebuke. It would seem as if our Lord's chief internal suffering had been his being misunderstood by the men that loved Him and whom He loved.

Besides the righteous indignation expressed in the rebuke to St. Peter, there are other passages in the Gospels where Christ expresses grief, if not anger, at being so sadly misunderstood. 'Incredulous and perverse generation, how long shall I be with you, how long shall I bear you?' The very men who come to Him with their sick to be healed doubt His power and His Mission. It might be said that the tragedy of the Gospels lies in that constant misunderstanding. There is a kind of ill will in Our Lord's surroundings which our Lord compares in one passage with the naughtiness and the sulkiness of children playing in the market-place. 'We played to you, and you would not sing; we piped to you, and you would not dance.'

Certain schools of religion in our own days take a pleasure in explaining Christ's unpopularity from political or social motives. Christ raised His voice against the rich and the powerful in favour of the poor, it is said. His unpopularity was like the unpopularity of a demagogue with the ruling party.

Such a view is strangely superficial. Our Lord was misunderstood by His own friends more than by anyone else. He rebuked the poor as sternly as He rebuked the rich. Many did not walk with Him any more, saying, 'This is a hard speech; who can bear it?' The hard speech was anything but a revolutionary speech: it was the announcement of the Holy Eucharist.

There was, in fact, not a single individual, with the exception of His mother, who had come into contact with Christ, who at one time or another was not a prey to doubts as to His real mission and character. His crucifixion was a scandal even to the most persevering friend. 'You all shall suffer scandal in me to-night.' Christ's life's effort seems to have been to gain the confidence of a few. Now, why is it that our Lord had such difficulty in gaining a following entirely devoted to Him, when it is the achievement of every agitator to gather round him in a few days crowds of men who believe in him blindly, and swear by him, ready to die for him or with him. There is not a trace of such overpowering ascendancy over man in our Lord's life. Doubt, suspicion, diffidence, are seen on every side. Peter alone boasts that he is ready to follow Him to prison and to death, and the Master meets His boast with a sad smile. ' I come in my Father's name, and you do not believe me. Somebody else will come in his own name, and you will believe him.'

Leaders of all sorts with human causes or human interests, coming in their own names, have done indeed what Christ could not do: they have had desperate followers. If the Gospels were the imagination of naïve men they would have represented their hero as a man of irresistible power over his followers; his manifold miracles would have been given as the explanation of a devotedness unto death on the part of the followers. Instead, we have miracles on the one hand, and unsurmountable diffidences on the other hand.

The explanation is this: Christ had no human cause to defend; he was no partisan; He came, as He says, in the name of His Father, with the fulness of truth, not with a political or social idea. He came with all ideas, and it would seem that the human mind has difficulties in trusting another mind that is not one-sided, but is complete and absolutely wise, taking in every view and every side of things. Man follows easily isolated impressions and ideas, as an animal follows irresistible instincts; but it is only highest culture that makes man love faithfully the fulness of truth, the truth of God in its multitudinousness of form and presentment. John the Baptist had no difficulty in getting a faithful following, in spite of his austerities; his disciples compare favourably with Christ's disciples in their loyalty to the leader. It was because John had a definite, an exclusive mode of life, whilst Christ required from His disciple every perfection of mind and heart.

Man's loyalty is always partisanship; faith in Christ, on the contrary, is intellectual culture and charity of the heart. To arrive at a perfect faith in Christ, man has to give up what it is most difficult to part with, his partisan attachments. The Jews by whom He was surrounded were passionate partisans; everyone expected a Christ that would be the glorification and triumph of his own partisan ideal; Christ goes back to the fundamental universal non-partisan principles of life and sanctity, and He is met from every side with angry looks because He does not take up the race with the fanatic and the zealot. The Holy Ghost is the Kingdom of God, not the triumph of the Jewish nationality—the Spirit of God that knows no boundaries; He is the Spirit of the Greek as well as of the Jew; He is the only movement Christ came to establish.

All popularities are popularities of parties; to substitute for party universal charity and love is the surest way to be misunderstood.

CHAPTER XXIX

THE CHRIST TRAGEDY

CHRIST'S career has all the characteristics of a tragedy; He was born to be the consolation of Israel, and He proved to be the child that is set for the fall and for the resurrection of many in Israel, and for a sign which shall be contradicted.[1]

Israel had been living in the hopes of a child conceived and born of the Virgin, bearing the glorious name of Emmanuel, to be a sign of God's omnipotent favour to His people in distress.

But, like many other long-expected scions of ruling houses, He proved to be His people's misfortune and curse: 'Let his blood be upon us, and upon our children.'[2]

History, so full of the cruellest tragedies, has no tragedy like the tragedy of Christ. The hope for which Israel lived became its curse through that awful misunderstanding which the Gospel calls blindness of heart. St. Paul has dramatised the terrible irony of things with the genius of a Sophocles

---

[1] St. Luke ii. 34.   [2] St. Matt. xxvii. 25.

in the Epistle to the Romans : ' I speak the truth in Christ, I lie not, my conscience bearing me witness in the Holy Ghost, that I have great sadness, a continual sorrow in my heart ; for I wished myself to be an anathema from Christ for my brethren who are my kinsmen, according to the flesh, who are Israelites, to whom belongeth the adoption as of children, and the glory, and the testimony, and the giving of the law, and the service of God, and the promises; whose are the fathers, and of whom is Christ, according to the flesh, who is over all things, God blessed for ever. . . .'[1] What then shall we say ? That the Gentiles who followed not after justice, have attained to justice, even the justice that is of faith ? But Israel, by following after the law of justice, is not come unto the law of justice. Why so ? Because they sought it not by faith, but as it were of works ; for they stumbled at the stumbling-stone, as it is written, Behold, I lay in Sion a stumbling-stone and a rock of scandal, and whosoever believeth in Him shall not be confounded.'[2] ' Brethren, the will of my heart indeed and my prayer to God is for them unto salvation ; for I bear them witness that they have a zeal of God, but not according to knowledge ; for they, not knowing the justice of God and seeking to establish their own, have not submitted themselves to the justice of God.'[3]

[1] Rom. ix. 1-5. [2] Rom. ix. 30-33. [3] Rom. x. 1-3.

But nothing would show more clearly the bitterness of the tragedy than St. Luke's picture in chapter xix. of his Gospel. 'And when Jesus drew near, seeing the city, He wept over it, saying, If thou also hadst known, and that in this thy day, the things that are to thy peace, but now they are hidden from thine eyes, for the days shall come upon thee, and thy enemies shall cast a trench about thee, and compass thee round, and straiten thee on every side, and beat thee flat to the ground, and thy children who are in thee ; and they shall not leave in thee a stone upon a stone, because thou hast not known the time of thy visitation.'

It may be said with perfect theological accuracy that what was the primary motive of Christ's coming was a tremendous failure, a failure which Christ tried to avert with all His might. We are too apt to think that Christ courted failure in order that prophecies might be fulfilled, and that His sacrifice on the Cross might become a possibility. No doubt it is difficult for our limited mind to see how an event which God has chosen to be the means of some great good does not become, through the fact of that divine choice, a necessary and unavoidable event, from which there is no escape ; and if efforts at escaping it are made, they look very much like so many sham movements. As it was written that Christ should die to save mankind, we find it difficult to believe that Christ's effort to win the Jewish nation to His love were efforts of tremendous sincerity.

He is very persistent in reminding His disciples of this His failure, in order to teach them not to be discouraged at their own future Apostolic failures; in fact, the memory of Christ's failure ought to keep the Christian from being ambitious even in his zeal for the Master. ' Amen, Amen, I say to you, the servant is not greater than his Lord, neither is the Apostle greater than he that sent him. If you know these things, you shall be blessed if you do them.'[1] ' If the world hate you, know you that it has hated me before you. If you had been of the world, the world would love its own; but because you are not of the world, but I have chosen you out of the world, therefore the world hateth you. Remember my word that I said to you, The servant is not greater than his master. If they have persecuted me, they will also persecute you; if they have kept my word, they will keep yours also.[2]

' And when they shall persecute you in this city, flee into another. Amen, I say to you, You shall not finish all the cities of Israel till the Son of man come. The disciple is not above the master, nor the servant above his lord. It is enough for the disciple that he be as his master, and the servant as his lord. If they have called the good

[1] St. John xiii. 16, 17.   [2] St. John xv. 18-20.

man of the house Beelzebub, how much more them of his household?'[1]

In this utterance we have an allusion to the saddest instance of Christ's powerlessness against Pharisaical envy, and no doubt the failure rankled deep in his heart. 'Then was offered to him one possessed with a devil, blind and dumb, and he healed him so that he spoke and saw; and all the multitude were amazed, and said, Is not this the Son of David? But the Pharisees, hearing it, said, This man casteth not out devils, but by Beelzebub the prince of the devils.' To have Himself recognised as the Son of David would have been Christ's triumph; to be the Son of David meant everything to the Jewish mind. But then there is the other extreme, the summit of moral depravation, the lowest depth of degradation—to be an associate of Beelzebub. Confronted by such consummate wickedness of thought, Christ speaks of the hopelessness of saving such men. 'Therefore I say to you, Every sin and blasphemy shall be forgiven men; but the blasphemy of the Spirit shall not be forgiven. And whoever shall speak a word against the Son of man, it shall be forgiven him; but he that shall speak against the Holy Ghost, it shall not be forgiven him, neither in this world nor in the world to come.'[2]

This attitude of the Pharisaical mind, even

[1] St. Matt. x. 23-25.   [2] St. Matt. xii. 31, 32.

THE CHRIST TRAGEDY

more than Christ's death, brings home to us the horror of the Christ tragedy. Repeatedly Our Lord makes it clear, both by word and deed, that He had it in His power to escape physically from the hands of His enemies, but nowhere do we find it said by Him that it was within His power to win His enemies to His love. He did all He could, and He failed. ' If I had not come and spoken to them, they would not have sinned; but now they have no excuse for their sin. He that hateth me hateth my Father also. If I had not done among them the works that no other man has done, they would not have sinned: but now they have both seen and hated both me and my Father. But that the word might be fulfilled which is written in their law, They have hated me without cause.' [1]

Twice St. Mark, when describing Christ's controversies with the Pharisees, hints at the feelings of this despairing sadness that clouded Christ's heart with regard to their spiritual state: ' And looking round about on them with anger, being grieved for the blindness of their hearts.' [2] ' And the Pharisees came forth, and began to question with him, asking him a sign from heaven, tempting him. And sighing deeply in his spirit he said, Why doth this generation ask a sign.' [3]

The sin against the Holy Ghost marked, if one

[1] St. John xv. 22-25. [2] St. Mark iii. 5.
[3] St. Mark viii. 11, 12.

may use this expression, the limits of Christ's spiritual power: He shrank back helpless; He became its victim, because the Pharisee, confirmed for ever in that state of mental perverseness, became the direct author of His crucifixion and His death. After the resurrection of Lazarus, some who had been the witnesses of the miracle went to the Pharisees and told them of the miracles that Jesus had done. 'The chief priests therefore and the Pharisees gathered a council, and said, What do we? for this man does many miracles. . . . From that day therefore they devised to put Him to death.'[1]

'Judas therefore, having received a band of soldiers and servants from the chief priests and the Pharisees, cometh thither with lanterns and torches and weapons.'[2]

The sin against the Holy Ghost is one of the facts of the New Testament most deserving of the attention of the critic and the theologian. It is a phenomenon that stands out in its hideous nakedness as prominently as Christ's cross itself, with this difference however, that the cross is surrounded with the halo of eternal hope, whilst the sin against the Holy Ghost is everlasting reprobation, started here on earth. It made the cross and got no blessings from it, but only curses; because blasphemy against the Son of man was turned into

[1] St. John xi. 47, 53.   [2] St. John xviii. 3.

THE CHRIST TRAGEDY

praise of the Son of man at the foot of the cross, whilst that dark blasphemer against the Holy Ghost, the Pharisee, and his confederates, blasphemed more than ever: 'And they that passed by blasphemed him, wagging their heads and saying, Vah, thou that destroyest the temple of God and in three days dost rebuild it, save thy own self. If thou be the Son of God, come down from the cross. In like manner also the chief priests, with the scribes and the ancients, mocking, said, He saved others; himself he cannot save. If he be the King of Israel, let him now come down from the cross, and we will believe him. He trusted in God; let him now deliver him, if he will have him: for he said, I am the Son of God.' [1]

This blasphemy is the strangest mental inconsequence: they admit the fact that He saved others, that He worked miracles; they make use of this uncontested power of His to deride His present apparent helplessness; the past signs of God's presence in Christ, which they admit, are made the occasion of this satanic gibe: 'He trusted in God; let him now deliver him, if he will have him.' For such perverseness there is no hope of return.

[1] St. Matt. xxvii. 39-43.

CHAPTER XXX

THE CHARACTER OF CHRIST

CHARACTER is the one element in the human individual that gives power over one's fellows.

It makes all other gifts useful; without it, the most brilliant mind is a mere toy in the hands of caprice.

Character binds our various gifts into one mighty organism, making them all into a full-grown body, capable of every effort.

Take one of the most brilliant of human minds that ever was, St. Paul: his intellect was of the highest rank. But at the same time, its very fierceness was a danger to its usefulness. But the one element that binds all his thoughts together is his intense earnestness and unselfishness of character. Whatever St. Paul says belongs not only to the permanent, but to the permanently living literature of mankind, precisely because you feel underneath it all a most potent character, in whom there is not a single weakness.

So with Christ: there is in Him His human

character. We cannot love Him with a lasting love until by meditation we have found out something of His manner and ways.

We know Christ to be the fulness of Godhead; we know Him to be the Wisdom of God. We know Him to be the Judge of the living and of the dead. We know Him to be the great wonder-worker. But all these magnificent, nay, infinite, attributes become a living, a fascinating power to us if once we have understood His character.

Not to understand His character makes such colossal gifts into a terror rather than into a consolation.

It is the old experience of mankind, in a higher way no doubt, yet it is the old experience.

You hear of a man who is making himself a name through brilliant gifts, through great activities—say, political activities. Perhaps that very brilliancy of gifts is irritating to you, looking at the man from a distance, looking at him as a stranger looks on another stranger. You think him haughty, selfish, unscrupulous, precisely because he is putting forward brilliant, dazzling, unusual gifts. Now if it be your chance or your good fortune one day to make the man's personal acquaintance, to be admitted amongst the circle of his friends, your prejudice goes in most cases, because you have come to see the man's character, you have found out how his brilliant gifts are reinforced by solid qualities; how he is a patient human sufferer after all; and the charm of his character makes you love the man whom unusual endowments had rendered suspect to you. To hate certain men, the surest way is to keep far from them. Love comes with the knowledge of their personal character.

Now, with Christ, there is what I might almost call the striking, the brilliant side of His Personality. He is a being on a colossal scale to us all. He is God; He is the Victor over Death and Hell. He comes in the power of His Father, with the angels of God, at the voice of the archangel, with the sound of the trumpet of God, to judge the living and the dead. His mortal life is full of mighty contrasts; His birth is amongst the angels; He is set for the rise and the fall of many. His death, again, is a tragedy on a colossal scale, with rent rocks, and darkness all over the earth, and the dead stirring in their graves. His resurrection is made known to the disciples by an angel whose countenance is like unto lightning. There would be the danger, and in fact there is the danger of such greatness producing nothing but wondering faith, when the proper and perfect attitude of Christ's disciple ought to be sweet and affectionate love, a friendship more gentle than the friendship of man for woman.

And spiritual experience teaches that those only rise above mere wondering faith who have taken the trouble of making Christ's personal acquaintance,

THE CHARACTER OF CHRIST

and thus have gained an insight into what I might almost call His private character, by studying closely His sacred Gospels, trying to find out the real meaning, the real intentions of Christ, in every one of His deeds and sayings. To quote one instance only. The tears shed over the sorrow of the widow who had lost her son, or the tears shed over the death of His own friend Lazarus, are as important an element in the comprehension of Christ's Personality as the miraculous resurrection of Easter. The one makes Him admirable, the other makes Him lovable. Or to keep to the Resurrection itself, Christ's interview with Mary Magdalene at the sepulchre, His ineffably sweet salutation to the holy women, when He met them, are as important as the glorious and overpowering apparition of the angel that announced the great victory over death. They reveal Christ's character, and they make of the ineffably sublime the ineffably human.

I am about to make use of a comparison which I hope no one will think a profanation if I use it in connection with so divine a Personality. Suppose history told us that Wellington, half an hour after the results of the battle of Waterloo had become a certainty to him, had been seen caressing children and having them on his knee, such a trait would act like some irresistible galvanic force, like some magic stream of life, turning the cast-iron statue of a superior man into a living being, with sparkling eyes, and smiling lips, and a rapturous atmosphere of humanity about him. You could not help loving the man. His character would have shown itself, uniting as by an electric flash the impalpable and intangible element of high genius, to turn them into the living waters of perfect humanity. I must once more crave the reader's pardon for using such human similes; but I am anxious to make him understand that up and down the Gospel narrative there are those traits, those flashes of humanity, which reveal Our Lord's character, and which unite all the sublimities of His wonderful Personality into the one sweet, most loving and most lovable Jesus of Nazareth—the Jesus of the city of flowers.

It is a study which we have to do ourselves, which every Christian who wants to grow in the personal love of Christ has to begin from the start. Nothing can replace in our spiritual life the constant perusal of the Gospel narrative with a view to treasure up the character-traits of the Son of God. The Gospels themselves are written in such wise as eminently to facilitate their study for even the simple and ignorant. They are a series of traits. The chronological order is made almost entirely subservient to the more important rôle of character portraiture. It is a sad thing that, with the multiplication of excellent exegetical works on the Gospels, our knowledge of Christ's intimate life is not growing apace. I am the very last man to withhold the due mede of praise from the productions of modern scholarship in its efforts to make the text of the Gospels clear, by submitting it to the ordinary canons of text interpretation. Such labours have all resulted in establishing the intrinsic antiquity, authenticity, and majesty of the Gospels. At the same time, it has to be admitted that the text of the Gospels can fulfil, and does fulfil, its main mission without the great scientific apparatus of modern scholarship. The Evangelists give us a picture of the Lord, such as they knew Him, and this picture every human creature is free to behold.

It would be too long a process to give what I consider to be character-traits of Christ, scattered as they are all over the four Gospels. I must ask the reader to do this himself, and certainly nothing could be more profitable to our souls than to write out for ourselves such a collection of sayings and acts as would endear Christ to us.

The Holy Ghost Himself has given us the key to Christ's personal character, in an immortally beautiful passage in the Prophet Isaias—a passage which has all the more importance as a character sketch of Christ, as the Evangelist St. Matthew quotes it amongst circumstances that show well that in it we have the main elements of Christ's natural disposition.

The passage is from the forty-second chapter of the Prophet Isaias. 'Behold my servant, I will uphold him : my elect, my soul delights in him : I have given my spirit upon him, he shall bring forth judgment to the gentiles. He shall not cry, nor have respect to person, neither shall his voice be heard abroad. The bruised reed he shall not break, and the smoking flax he shall not quench : he shall bring forth judgment unto truth. He shall not be sad, nor troublesome, till he set judgment in the earth ; and the islands shall wait for his law.'[1]

St. Matthew quotes it in common with a series of Pharisaical fault-findings, and Christ's endeavour to spare their feelings. 'At that time Jesus went through the corn on the sabbath : and his disciples being hungry, began to pluck the ears, and to eat. And the Pharisees seeing them, said to him : Behold thy disciples do that which is not lawful to do on the sabbath day. But he said to them : Have you not read what David did when he was hungry, and they that were with him : How he entered into the house of God, and did eat the loaves of proposition, which it was not lawful for him to eat, nor for them that were with him, but for the priests only ? Or have ye not read in the law, that on the sabbath days the priests in the temple break the sabbath, and are without blame ? But I tell you that there is here a greater than the temple. And if you knew what this meaneth : I will have mercy, and not sacrifice : you would never have condemned the

[1] Is. xlii. 1-4.

innocent. For the Son of man is Lord even of the sabbath. And when he had passed from thence, he came into their synagogue. And behold there was a man who had a withered hand, and they asked him, saying: Is it lawful to heal on the sabbath days? that they might accuse him. But he said to them: What man shall there be among you, that hath one sheep: and if the same fall into a pit on the sabbath day, will he not take hold on it and lift it up? How much better is a man than a sheep? Therefore it is lawful to do a good deed on the sabbath day. Then he saith to the man: Stretch forth thy hand; and he stretched it forth, and it was restored to health even as the other. And the Pharisees going out made a consultation against him, how they might destroy him. But Jesus, knowing it, retired from thence: and many followed him, and he healed them all. And he charged them that they should not make him known. That it might be fulfilled which was spoken by Isaias the prophet, saying: Behold my servant whom I have chosen, my beloved in whom my soul hath been well pleased. I will put my spirit upon him, and he shall shew judgment to the Gentiles. He shall not contend, nor cry out, neither shall any man hear his voice in the streets. The bruised reed he shall not break: and smoking flax he shall not extinguish: till he send forth judgment unto victory. And in his name the Gentile shall hope.'

We know what is meant when it is said of anyone that he is regardless of his fellow man's feelings and interests. Regardlessness is the incapacity or the unwillingness practically to admit the fact that our fellow creatures are creatures of flesh and blood like ourselves, that the humblest of them, if their heart be crushed, will groan, and that from their skins will purl forth red, warm, human blood, if they be pricked, just as it is with ourselves. One can be regardless from high motives as well as from low motives, and the motive does not change the case. One may be a ' bully ' in the pursuit of offices and lucre, and one may be a ' bully ' in the pursuit of an ideal, even a spiritual ideal. Even a good man may become so absorbed with some spiritual scheme as to make men, as well as things, subservient to it, making mere tools of them for the furtherance of the scheme, with a view to some general effect, entirely regardless of the rights, the happiness, the needs of the individual. The Pharisee is an instance. Man with him does not count any more ; it is the law, the ideal, the general effect that is everything.

Now it is precisely in this that Christ differs, *toto coelo*, from the spiritual bully called the Pharisee. With Our Lord the ideal is the happiness, the salvation, the well-being of the individual soul. This divine ' regardfulness ' both for the rights and possibilities of every human being is essentially His character.

He does not carry His disciples along with Him, striding on rapidly, towards a high, abstract goal. Such may be the conduct of a human leader. Nor does He put before them anything great to achieve, except to love Him, to be faithful to Him, and give faithful testimony of Him when the time comes. He drives back energetically any mere ideal, the ideal of a kingdom, the ideal of some great spiritual estate. The ideal is that they love Him, that they love each other, that they believe in His love for them. His Personality is the ideal. He considers that His life's work is well done, because they have come to believe in Him and to love Him. Most great men have failed in this point. Their schemes have been their idols, and they have utilised the best men merely as tools. And as a consequence no one remained behind to love them or weep over their death.

Christ is God indeed, Christ has all knowledge and all power; He has all things given into His hands. But all these gifts He uses in order to give eternal life to the humblest and poorest, in order that He may be loved by the simplest, in order that He may strengthen the weak reed, in order that He may rekindle the poor smoking flax. ' Before the festival day of the pasch, Jesus knowing that his hour was come, that he should pass out of this world to the Father: having loved his own who were in the world, he loved them unto the end. And when supper was done (the devil having now put into the heart of Judas Iscariot, the son of Simon, to betray him), knowing that the Father had given him all things into his hands, and that he came from God, and goeth to God ; he riseth from supper, and layeth aside his garments, and having taken a towel, girded himself. After that, he putteth water into a basin, and began to wash the feet of the disciples, and to wipe them with the towel wherewith he was girded.'[1]

[1] St. John xiii. 1-5.

CHAPTER XXXI

CHRIST'S PLACE IN THE WORLD

IT is an indisputable fact that Christ has become part of the psychology of many different races. He has entered into the depths of their mentality. No one but a madman could deny this extraordinary enthroning of the Christ ideal in the human mind of races most diversified. No critic of a race's mentality would be forgiven if he ignored that great element, Christ. It is more than mere religiousness; it is more than a doctrinal grip on theories; it is more than a conscience; it is something intensely personal; it is essentially the conscience of One outside the individual, yet deeply concerned with the life of the individual; it is of One who is a historic personality, and has at the same time the pliability of an ideal. No dream of even a Celtic imagination was less limited in its potentiality than is the Christ idea of the Christian races; at the same time see the wondrous individuality of that idea. We may differ, since the days of Protestantism, as to the practical subjective and objective means of getting at Christ, and renewing Christ in our own lives. But as for the view of Christ, taken as a whole, there is little difference between Catholic and Protestant races.

It would be as unwise as it would be unnecessary to minimise the mental differences, say, between an English evangelical and a French nun. In religious temperament they are the two antipodes ; but in the love of the Master they are one and the same. No one could be uncharitable enough to suspect the English evangelical of hypocrisy ; no one would ever dream of accusing the sweet-faced, berosaried inhabitant of a French nunnery of insincerity. The two are worlds apart in their religious temperament ; at the same time, their life in Christ whenever it expresses itself does so in identical language.

We have here another phenomenon worthy of the thinker's attention : how Christ's person has remained practically unimpaired in the Christian conscience in that great upheaval of Christian sentiment, in that great split of the Church He founded, in that great division of minds as to the best road of going to Him, called the Reformation. If anything were required to show the extent of the hold Christ has on His predilect races, this circumstance would show it. For the breach between the Protestant mind and the Catholic mind is profound ; it is almost incurable. But the gulf is not in what the Master is felt to be to man, but in the practical conception of what man ought to be to the Master. The French nun conceives herself to be Christ's bride, and she sacrifices herself even as Christ was sacrificed.

The English evangelical thinks more of Christ's benefaction to him than of an equal return of blood for blood.

Various races have expressed Christ variously. We need not make this the cause of scepticism. There is such multitudinousness and such profundity in Christ's character as to warrant the most various expressions of His life. At one time His theological, His divine side will appeal more to the mind of man. The first centuries are an instance of that. Then His crucifixion will be the most common feature associated with Him; the Middle Ages lived on the height of Calvary. At other periods His personal love is the foremost thought with the pious. The best explanation of those varieties is the ordinary psychological explanation: such views of Christ suit the temper of the period. Christ has all the elasticity of an abstract ideal; the created mind that conceives Him shapes Him to the image of its own higher and purer part. Yet, by doing so, the created mind holds more than an empty ideal; it holds a true substance, because Christ is all that in Himself.

It is one of the results of spiritual education

to revere the way in which each soul loves Christ, speaks to Christ, and speaks of Christ, whilst making use of one's liberty to approach Him differently, there being no impiety in not joining in specialised views of Him, even if such views are for the time being the attraction and the devotion of the greater number.

Few there are who express to themselves Christ wholly; it may even be questioned whether anyone can do it: I mean expressing Him not in His innate, interior state of being—for no finite mind could do that—but expressing Him in the fulness of His state, such as faith teaches Him to be.

There is nothing one ought to be more careful about than to accuse any Christian of holding an imperfect, a defective view of Christ. For no Christian ever limits Christ in his heart and mind. He grasps what he can; he depicts Him to himself according to his need and temper of mind. He hardly ever draws the line sharply. He feels that He is a Man, but a Man with an endless reserve of the Higher Life, with the inclusion of Divinity itself. Even if the uneducated were to affirm that he does not believe Christ to be God, I should still hesitate in my heart to believe him, and give my brother the benefit of the doubt. For in his ignorance, to deny that Christ is God is not the same as to disbelieve the Incarnation; most likely, if it were put to him that Christ is God without ceasing to be man, this view of the Godhead, as being a kind of glorious reserve in Christ's manhood, would exactly express his own slumbering thoughts.

Christ could not be the living Power He is without deeply modifying the ethical sense of the nations that worship Him. There are certain precepts which we all speak of as precepts of the Gospel, because they are so strongly emphasised in the Sacred Gospels. But precepts alone would not be enough to create a new ethical sense of a universal character.

Ethical sense, in a healthy and normal state, gives peace to those that possess it and conform to it in practice. It is part of man's innermost nature, it belongs to the vital elements of his being. No set of precepts, however wise, could create the ethical sense.

Precepts, in order to be living things, must be expressions of the hidden ethical sense of man; they do not cross his aspirations, they merely elevate them. Now, the lessons of history are that wherever the name of Christ is alive, there we find profound ethical assurance and certainty, besides ethical simplicity and directness, all of which results in great ethical peace.

There is, in practice, very little difference between the Utopian state of ethical perfection and Gospel perfection. The kindliest, purest, strongest man of Utopia is not kinder, purer, and stronger than the perfect disciple of Christ. Do we not all dream of Christian nations as living in simplicity amongst Nature's pure beauties, and endowed with every manliness that comes, as it were, from close contact with Nature?

Has not Christianity flourished most luxuriantly amongst the ethically healthiest races of the world, and is not decline in a nation's ethical healthiness also decline in a nation's Christianity? All that ethical healthiness is necessarily Christ's property: it is His most precious possession here on earth; it is part of His Kingdom, and He has proved Himself to be the Living God through the fact that He has grafted Himself so easily, and as it were so naturally, on the purest ethical sense the world does possess.

I do not think that there could be a movement in the world more anti-Christian than that of separating the ethical sense of mankind from Christ, representing Christ as antagonistic to man's ethical sense, and trying to make the ethical sense self-sufficient.

Christ is the King of Peace, because in Him man's ethical needs are satisfied. He has not brought a law only; He has brought more. He has brought life.

It is very strange that the deepest laws of human nature—which are not so much laws as elements of life—have come to be considered as the elementary precepts of Christianity. We speak of the man who violates them in his own person as of a bad Christian; and, as I remarked a moment ago, in practice there is no difference between the voice of Nature and the voice of Christ.

In practice, and in the conscience of men, Christ has become the voice of Nature. A man is acting against the precepts of Christ, not only when he does not forgive his enemy, but also when he is intemperate or lazy. The purest love, as well as the renouncement of all things sensual, is Christ's life; and nothing could be more hurtful to the cause of Christianity than to make of renouncement Christ's law, and of Nature's true and legitimate joys the world's law. They are both Christ's, making one and the same life in a variety of functions. The mystical nuptials of the cloistered virgin and the pure love of conjugal life are equally Christian in character, though they may represent a difference of spiritual perfection. A founder of religion, not wholly divine, could not have hit on the secret of thus making Nature's purities part of His own sanctity, in the conscience of men and women. Such a founder of mere human wisdom would have singled out one ethical point, one ascetical practice, as the special badge for his followers.

Not so Christ, such a Christ as has lived amongst the nations for centuries. He has become to them the fulness of every moral perfection, the ideal of every purity; He rebukes them in their hearts for every kind of transgression.

Christ, and 'He crucified,' is to mankind profound ethical peace. If there is no peace for the wicked, there is no peace either for the man who has lost the just balance in the practice of good. The fanatic looks as empty of the peace of God as the profligate himself. There is no sweet harmony in his soul, there is no joyfulness in his eyes however good his intentions may be. He is without peace in Himself, and he is the enemy of his neighbour's peace.

It would be almost impossible, humanly speaking, to have as one's ethical ideal a God crucified, without the danger of an extreme ethical severity, without a fanatical courting of the harrowing and the dreadful. Yet, Christ crucified has been a greater source of joyful peace than any other ethical ideal. This comes from the divinely rational measure of Christ's crucifixion.

Christ's cross is the wisdom of God; its measure is God's prudence, if the word 'prudence' be applicable to the acts of God. There is no wanton display of physical endurance in Christ's Passion; there is no inhuman contempt for physical pain; but there is a strong, patient bearing of so much pain as was indispensable to achieve a spiritual result. Every pang of that divine pain had its own object in view, and once the object attained, the pain was thrown away as a tool that burns the hand that uses it. Christ's Passion was indeed wrapped up in the sweetness of God's Wisdom.

Christ crucified is the source of the ever-refreshing stream of human life, because His crucifixion, taking place in the very centre, as it were, of God's wisdom and prudence, is an eternal delight to the minds that contemplate it. It is the most wondrous proportion between means and end; it was Christ's highest moment of mortal and created spiritual life; and whilst his lips were parched with the thirst of his agony, His spirit was quickened within Himself, and thus refreshed it went forth into the world of spirits, to announce the good news of the redemption to those spirits that had been incredulous in the days of Noah.

Christ suffered, as a Divine Person ought to suffer, with patient wisdom, yielding reluctantly to the encroachment of pain on His own natural happiness, yet yielding bravely, because yielding meant salvation to the souls He carried in the bosom of His love.

CHAPTER XXXII

CHRIST AND THE WORLD'S PROGRESS

IT would be the greatest theological mistake to consider Christ's humanity merely as a vessel of rare material in which Divinity dwells in a state of repose, as in a consecrated tabernacle. On the contrary, the humanity of Christ is raised through that sublime indwelling to the highest and farthest realisation of all the potentialities of humanity. Christ is manhood made exceedingly great in itself through the participation of Personal Godhead. Godhead has achieved in Christ an elevation of humanity such as to bewilder the heavenly intelligences. Any raising up, therefore, of mankind is strictly within the movement and the grace of Hypostatic Union.

To confine the raising up merely to the internal graces, to the directly mystical part of man, would not do justice to the great fact that God became man. The advancement of humanity on every possible line of progress, spiritual, mystical, intellectual, and material, is the only true and adequate view of the practical meaning of the Incarnation for mankind. There is indeed in Christ's personal life a preponderance of the spiritual and mystical, a constant reminding of the one important thing —salvation of one's soul. In Himself He demonstrates that temporal failure is of small account, in order to carry out the great Atonement. But there is no condemnation of the material order of things, there is no spiritual or mystical one-sidedness. There is no such ascetical view of the life of sanctity with Him as to make it unlikely *a priori* that a great temporal empire might be based on the principles of the Gospel—an empire impregnated in practical administration with the Spirit of Christ.

No abuse of temporal things or intellectual progress by man can ever counterbalance the fact that Eternal Wisdom and Eternal Power became man, making use of temporal things, and thinking in a human intelligence, and making therefore through the infinite superiority of His one Personality over the whole human crowd His use of temporal things, and His knowledge of created secrets, an unassailable title to the possession of the earth. If the earth belongs by right to the best, who has a firmer hold on it than the One who is infinitely better than His fellows? It is true that intimacy with, and love for, the mystical life in Christ frequently begets in simple souls a kind of suspicion of all temporal progress as being a hiding and an obscuring of Christ's sovereignty. Such suspicions are certainly not the fulness of the spirit of Christian wisdom. Why should civilisation be a danger to the Christ ideal? A Utopian age would still fall short of the human possibilities contained in the personal union of the Second Person of the Trinity with human nature in Christ.

It is not at all certain that a lower state of civilisation is more favourable to the prosperity of Christian faith than a highly advanced civilisation. It would be very ungenerous of us to think that the Man-God would feel ill at ease in a world full of enlightenment and philanthropy. Some of us seem to have a lurking fear lest the civilisation initiated by Christian ideals should outgrow those very ideals, and that it should become greater than the Christ who founded it. This is a very ungracious attitude of mind, and one that nothing in Christ's mortal life, nothing in our Christology, justifies.

That Christ chose poverty, and failure, and the cross is no indication that He abdicated that sovereignty over the world that is His from the simple fact that He is the one being in whom manhood is united to Godhead itself, through oneness of personality.

In His teaching He refers to Himself as the

king of the world, to whom all power has been given. His sayings concerning detachment from temporal things are such as might well be taken to heart by the director of some mighty business in the twentieth century, without such admonitions interfering with the man's practical usefulness. The eight beatitudes are a possible code of spirituality for every conceivable state of human life and every sort of temporal enterprise that is honest in itself. Riches, which were an insurmountable obstacle to the acceptance of the kingdom of God, have become the object of a special act of God's power, in Christ, to take from them their hardening influence. 'Then Jesus said to his disciples: Amen I say to you, that a rich man shall hardly enter into the kingdom of heaven. And again I say to you, It is easier for a camel to pass through the eye of a needle than for a rich man to enter the kingdom of heaven. And when they had heard this the disciples wondered very much, saying: Who then can be saved? And Jesus beholding said to them, With men this is impossible; but with God all things are possible.'[1]

It is true that Christ calls some of His followers to the imitation of His own intensely spiritual life—a life that discards as far as possible the use of temporal things. But Christian tradition has always considered such calls to be a special grace,

[1] St. Matt. xix. 23-26.

a special vocation, and nothing warrants the assertion that it was Christ's intention that the majority of those that receive His name are meant to follow this more detached mode of life. Those that do renounce all things will always be, as they have always been, a very small minority of the Christian people. Above all, the practice of what is called 'Evangelical perfection '—i.e. of that external renunciation of temporal things—if properly understood, far from being an obstacle to the progress of human civilisation, has been one of its most potent levers of action. It is a constant principle of our Christology that Christ adopted a life of comparative poverty and of exclusively spiritual powers from His own choice. It was one of the many courses He could have followed. He had in Him such powers as would have made Him the first and greatest in every line of human power and influence. Hypostatic Union includes it all, and much more. The choice Christ made of what might be termed an exclusively spiritual career ought not to make us forget how much else there was in Him, not indeed in a state of dormancy, but in a state of expectation, to become active under other circumstances, when the work of His spiritual Atonement would be accomplished.

CHAPTER XXXIII

THE POWER OF CHRIST

Christ's Person is the real inwardness of the Church. The Church, in the words of St. Paul, is Christ's body and the fulness of Him who is filled all in all.[1]

All the powers of the Church, all her rights, all her duties are conditioned by this personality-view of Christ. The Church has no authority outside it, has no mission besides it. As a matter of fact, Christ's Personality and His Church are inseparable concepts; they are what is called in logic convertible concepts—one concept includes the other. The Church is not an empire of which Christ is the King, because an empire may be composed of free men and slaves; the Church is, on the contrary, the union of souls in Christ. There may be in the Church administrative power, at least in the Church here on earth; but this power, again, is conditioned in its operations and in its extent by the personal relations of souls with

[1] Eph. i. 23.

Christ. The power is given to Peter to win souls to Christ, and keep souls in Christ, and his power is so great precisely because the aim of it all is so great—the restoration of all things in Christ.

If the power of the Catholic Church or, for the matter of that, of the Papacy were to exert itself for objects entirely outside that personal relation of souls with Christ, the abuse of power would bring its Nemesis very swiftly in the way of some great religious cataclysm. The nature of ecclesiastical power may assume a stern mood, but its sternness can never be anything but a reflection of Christ's own merciful severities. ' Behold, this is the third time I am coming to you. In the mouth of two or three witnesses shall every word stand. I have told before, and foretell, as present, and now absent, to them that sinned before, and to all the rest, that if I come again I will not spare. Do you seek a proof of Christ that speaketh in me, who towards you is not weak, but is mighty in you ? For although he was crucified through weakness, yet he liveth by the power of God. For we also are weak in him ; but we shall live with him by the power of God towards you. Try your own selves if you be in the faith ; prove ye yourselves. Know you not your own selves, that Christ Jesus is in you, unless perhaps you be reprobates ? But I trust that you shall know that we are not reprobates. Now we pray God, that you may do no evil, not that we may appear approved, but that you may do that which is good, and that we may be as reprobates. For we can do nothing against the truth, but for the truth. For we rejoice, that we are weak, and you are strong: This also we pray for, your perfection. Therefore I write these things, being absent, that, being present, I may not deal more severely, according to the power which the Lord hath given me unto edification, and not unto destruction. For the rest, brethren, rejoice, be perfect, take exhortation, be of one mind, have peace ; and the God of peace and of love shall be with you. Salute one another with a holy kiss. All the saints salute you.'[1]

[1] 2 Cor. xiii. 1-13.

CHAPTER XXXIV

THE FINDING OF CHRIST

THE dominion which the Almighty gave to man at the beginning of all things over 'the fishes of the sea and the fowls of the air and the beasts and the whole earth, and every creeping creature that moveth upon the earth,'[1] is not only inexhaustible in its resources, but also unlimited in its possible developments. Mother Earth whilst feeding her children is not always equally known by her children, and perhaps the race of men that will know her perfectly is not to come for thousands of years yet; but when such a race actually does come, the earth it will tread will not be a different earth from the one on which we move. Their dwellings will stand on the same ground as was tenanted by the primitive man with his savage hut. Now this is a parable in order to convey the attitude of the human race, or even of Christian races, towards the God-man, towards the second Adam, the great foundation, as St. Paul calls Him, on which we all build up our spiritual dwelling.

[1] Gen. i. 26.

Christ is to be conquered by the world as the earth is to be conquered by man. We have to find out His treasures, His secrets, His spirit, and the success of that conquest has as many phases as man's conquest of the earth. There never was any intermittence in the earth's subjugation by man; but how different has been man's dominion at various periods! So Christ has always been possessed by man; but how different has been at various times that blessed possession of Him!

To some minds it may be a scandal to find Christ is loved and comprehended so spasmodically, with such variability; yet such is exactly the fate of creation in general. Christ is God's great spiritual creation, more wonderful than any material creation; why should we be surprised at the endless flow and ebb of the human mind and the human heart with regard to Him? He must be contradicted as well as loved. He must be misunderstood as well as hailed with hosannas. He must be the sweet food of the world as well as the world's terror. He is the fulness of God's creation; we go in and go out in Him, and we find pasture in Him, according to our taste and talent. That wonderful continuity of His spirit and truth, the Catholic Church, does not alter the fact that Christ is man's conquest with a great variety of success; for even inside the Catholic Church the practical comprehension of His spirit and the practical application of His great law of love has its periods of savage primitiveness, and its periods of high civilisation, to speak metaphorically. Faith in Him is like the unchanging earth; sanctity in Him, with its accompanying gift of wisdom and understanding, admits of endless developments, failures, changes, and triumphs.

History speaks of different civilisations as well as of the differences between barbarity and civilisation. Some of the greatest civilisations seem to be older than all known forms of barbarity; nothing prevents our thinking in that way of God's great spiritual creation—Christ. The earliest record of man's conquest of Christ is high sanctity —the sanctity of the primitive Church. There were other sanctities, or rather other periods of sanctity —sanctity being the same essentially at bottom, yet with differences that are as great as the differences between various civilisations. Oneness of spirituality is not monotony of spirituality, and provided it be the same Christ, the same Faith, the same spirit of God, even the strictest orthodoxy will welcome any fresh manifestation of man's conquest of Christ.

Christ is not like men—and heaven knows how many such men there are—who are all front with nothing behind, who are seen through at a glance and put away with as much thought about them as about common glass; they are not the men that ever will be contradicted or misunderstood.

Christ is the man behind whose human front there is the infinite Godhead, the man who speaks not of the present hour only but of the end of the world.

'And he said: So is the kingdom of God as if a man should cast seed into the earth, and should sleep, and rise night and day, and the seed should spring and grow up whilst he knoweth not.'[1]

[1] St. Mark iv. 26, 27.

CHAPTER XXXV

CHRIST THE FATHER OF THE WORLD TO COME

Christ's religion is indeed a religion of the present world; it has finality in this world, though it has not its ultimate finality here. It gives happiness here on earth, though the happiness it gives is not ultimate happiness.

Such indeed are the advantages of Christian spirituality that no better spirituality could be devised for a race who would have no higher world to look forward to, as Christian ethics combine in giving to human life the highest sum of happiness.

The purpose of Christianity is sanctification, which means everything holy and true and beautiful. Its end is life everlasting, not indeed in the sense of its having no other interests except the interests of the invisible world, but in the sense of its sanctification being such as to bear everlasting fruits.

If the invisible world were Christianity's first and last finality, there might be the danger of exaggerated other-worldliness. The end and finality of Christianity is a sanctity which must needs take into account the present world; but eternal life is a natural result.

It may be said indeed that a desire for heavenly glory is part of sanctity. But it is not a part of the effort of sanctity—for who could make an effort to ascend to heaven?—but it is the natural consciousness that our present life sanctity finds its consummation in eternal glory. This is why we find in Christian spirituality the double phenomenon of Christ being present with us, filling our hearts with His love, and of that kind of yearning for the absent friend whom we hope to find in heaven. No more incomplete view of Christianity could be given than to define it a striving after a Christ who lives in the heavenly world. Christianity is life with Christ here on earth, and where highest sanctity has flourished, there has been the greatest actual presence of our Lord.

The question might be asked how in practice a religion would shape the minds and hearts of men if that religion had no finality in this world, but had it all in the next? To say the least, it would reduce everything human to the level of merely utilitarian means; it could not love anything here on earth for its own sake; it would be the dwarfing and warping of every human generosity; and no doubt with logical minds the disaster would go farther still, as the conviction would grow stronger that man has no direct means of ascending into heaven. But such is not Catholicism. It is an effort at human spirituality, at human sanctity, at a perfection to be acquired here in life. Its eternal results are not indeed indifferent to the saint; they are of the utmost importance to him, as his sanctification is essentially the perfection of his own immortal, never-dying soul. But it may be asserted quite safely that even with the greatest saint the thought of his going to heaven is only one of many thoughts, kept in its proper place by the more urgent and more active thoughts of doing the deeds of charity, of finding Christ in his own heart, of speaking with Him, and of being happy in His company.

The thought of heaven itself has always been considered as one of the main considerations to make the present life happy and perfect. It helps sanctity; but our efforts are not for the heavenly mansions, our efforts are for sanctity. Over and over again we find in Christ's religion, such as experience shows it to be, this wonderful balance of transcending philosophical wisdom: the crucified God teaches merciful tenderness for physical suffering; the Word that is in the bosom of the Father is the most perfect human being reigning in heaven at the right hand of the Father; His religion is the religion of the present world's happiness. Besides His throne in heaven He has His real presence in the Eucharist, and the unsatisfied craving of highest Christian sanctity is not so much of finding Him as of seeing Him, because sanctity has found Him already, but being of this world it has not seen Him yet.

The relation between sanctity here in life and eternal life might be considered from various points of view. Just now I want to insist on the psychological point of view—I mean the attitude of the Christian saint towards the blessedness of heaven. It is certain that no saint has any experimental knowledge of what awaits him in heaven; his desires for heaven, whatever they may be, are not of the things he has tasted and wants to taste again; even when most intense, those desires are immensely inferior to the excellency of the thing. To have a desire for heaven proportionate to the excellency of the heavenly bliss, one ought to imagine an elect who has lived in heaven and has come out of it again, back to mortal life—a supposition that is evidently contradictory in its terms. The saint's attitude therefore towards heaven is not, and never could be, the attitude of the man who is in search of a happiness he knows experimentally. It may be doubted whether it is at all possible to strive for an unknown thing; one might wait for it, wondering all the time what it will be, but striving for it with eagerness of mind and heart does not seem possible. This is why Christian sanctity is, essentially, an effort to possess Christ, to taste His sweetness, because, though He may not be fully known, He is not unknown. It may be said that every stage of sanctity has a realisation of Christ's Presence that gives it there and then entire satisfaction.

But heaven and its glorious mysteries are always beyond man's realisation. They are never to him a possession here on earth as Christ is. Christ is a kingdom within ourselves, heaven is a kingdom outside ourselves, and it is the inward kingdom that makes Christ's soldier happy in all his battles.

I do not think high spiritual life to be at all possible without that kingdom of God within us, whose peace surpasseth all understanding. To put it more clearly still, a spiritual system with no results in this life, with no gain in this life but merely as an effort towards and an expectation of a life after death, would be a great psychological blunder. Our Lord's religion is no such blunder.

CHAPTER XXXVI

THE LINK BETWEEN CHRIST'S MORTAL LIFE AND THE EUCHARIST

CHRIST'S real Presence in the Blessed Eucharist and His continued sacrifice on the altars of the Catholic Church at mass stamp His Personality with an originality as great as is Hypostatic Union. The Christian Eucharist, under its twofold aspect of food and sacrifice, is an inimitable concept ; by itself it would suffice to render Christianity unfit for the classification of Comparative Religion.

The Christ of the Eucharist has been made the object of a sort of specialisation in theology. Scholastic treatises on the wonderful sacrament and the not less wonderful sacrifice are as comprehensive and as important as the treatises on the Incarnation itself. Here I am concerned with one aspect only of that great spiritual marvel : the relation between Christ's mortal life and Christ's eucharistic life. All the moral perfection, all the sanctity, all the merit, all the atonement of which the God-man is capable were consummated in His one mortal life.

Christ is no exception to the great law of finality, which seems an inherent element of human life. How, then, are we to view this prolonged existence of Christ on earth ? How are we to view that endless repetition of His sacrifice from sunrise to sunset, on the altars of the Church, to the end of the world ? The measure of our redemption was full when Christ had shed the last drop of His blood ; how then this repetition in millions and milliards ? It will seem a paradox, yet it is the truest way to state the matter. The eucharistic renewing of Christ's death is a result of that infinite fulness of redemption that is in Christ's mortal life. Because Christ merited infinitely, merited and atoned with a luxuriant superabundance, we have the real Presence, we have the daily sacrifice of the Christian altar. For we ought to remember that the Eucharist itself is the result of Christ's merits, that through the sanctity of His life and death He gained for us the wonder of wonders : the Eucharistic Transubstantiation and its inherent sacrifice.

The Eucharist is the Christian's greatest privilege simply because It enables Him to enter into direct and physical communion with Christ's life and death. And this privilege Christ merited for His faithful, through the excess of His atoning love. To detach the Eucharist from Christ's mortal life would be the greatest aberration in the things of Christ. From the very beginning of the controversies about Christ's Divine Personality, the orthodox theologians challenged Nestorius to explain the Christian Eucharist without Divine Personality. How could we eat the flesh of one who is not God? Between Hypostatic Union and Transubstantiation the relation is most intimate, and most likely it implies contradiction that a human organism that has not Divine Being should be the physical food of spirits, in the supernatural order of things. After all, it is merely the *instrumentum conjunctum Divinitatis* in its highest manifestation.

But though we know little as to the aptitude which Christ's humanity gained to be the Eucharist of the Christian people through its life and death, yet the whole genius of our theology warrants the supposition that Christ became fit most eminently for this rôle through His life and death. His mortal career gave Him consummate fitness, in every sense, to be the author of life to souls.

Now, as ' life ' is essentially a personal relation with Him, the great object of all the meritoriousness of His sanctity was union with Himself; He merited this, that we should be in Him, and He in us. The Eucharist is the grandest and truest result of His holiness, as it is the grandest and truest union with the Person of Christ. All sacraments derive their spiritual powers from Christ's death. That one of them, instead of merely containing Christ's grace, contains Christ Himself only goes to show the efficacy of Christ's death. In the Eucharist, the Personality, which is the pivot of Christianity, has become not only a centre and a source of grace, but a means of grace.

The protestant argument against the Eucharist in general, and the Sacrifice of the Mass in particular, based on the all-sufficiency of the sacrifice of Calvary, would be best met by emphatic insistence, not only on the all-sufficiency, but on the infinite superabundance of it. All-sufficiency in the protestant mind applies to the work of Christ; it never means to the protestant all-sufficiency of mystical contact of souls with the great sacrifice. We grant him the all-sufficiency he knows of; we grant it more liberally than the protestant does; we grant an all-sufficiency of work so great that it breaks its limits, and from an all-sufficiency of work it becomes an all-sufficiency of contact of a most real nature.

CHAPTER XXXVII

THE MAJESTY OF THE EUCHARISTIC PRESENCE

PRESENCE means the existence of a being in a given part of the material universe. When we speak of presence, we must of necessity imply a certain position or attitude with regard to a material world.

If there were no matter, but only spirits, there could be no question of either presence or absence; there would be question only of distinct spiritual individualities, which would be neither near nor distant with regard to each other, but would exist each one by itself, having power to admit co-existing spirits into communication with its own intellectual life, or exclude them.

Presence and absence are essentially and radically connected with space, and space is connected with matter.

Now, though a spirit could not be said to be present or absent, with regard to a fellow spirit, if they remained both outside the material world, they are present or absent from each other on account of the material world. For one spirit may be in one part of the material world, and another spirit in another part of the material world, and then there is real distance between the two.

But how and why is a spirit in the material universe when his nature is so very immaterial?

The answer is this. A spirit is said to be in a certain place of the material universe, simply and solely because he exerts certain activities, produces certain effects, in that place, or on the material thing of that place, or even on the spiritual thing already connected, in a similar way, with that place.

If the spirit stops exerting his activity in the way mentioned, this very cessation of activity is in itself infinite distance from the spot where he was truly the instant before. The spirit comes and goes, not through movement, as a bodily thing, but through action or cessation of action on a bodily thing.

God and the angels are present in this way. Therefore, if a spirit can exert his activities on various parts of the universe at the same time, he is truly present at the same time to those various parts of the universe.

The more perfect a spirit, the more numerous are the points of the universe to which he can be present at the same time.

God, who is a spirit of infinite perfection, is accordingly present at the same time to every

THE EUCHARISTIC PRESENCE 253

point of the material universe, as every point of the material universe wants His sustaining power.

The human soul, in its present state at least, is the last and lowest amongst the spirits. Its main activity is to give life to the body, therefore it cannot be outside the individual body.

So much for the presence of spirits. It is a noble attribute of theirs; it is the majesty of their spirituality. They can be really present to the lowliest sort of matter, and yet remain infinitely superior to it. They are not contaminated by matter, but they invest matter with their sweet activity.

Coming now to the presence of bodies, in the material universe their being present anywhere comes from their imperfection, not their perfection; for their presence is such that they cannot help being present.

A body must of necessity occupy one given point of space in the material universe, and when the body occupies one given point of the material universe, it cannot be outside this one point at the same time. It is the subjection of a bodily creature which is the slave of space, whilst a spirit is the king over space.

It is true our glorified bodies in heaven, and above all the glorified body of Our Lord, are given wonderful powers of agility, so as to transport themselves from one spot to the other of the material world with the rapidity of thought. It is a certain liberation from the subjection to space. Yet even then it will be impossible for the glorified body to be at the same time in two places.

Now the wonder of wonders in the matter of presence, a majesty of presence almost akin to the majesty of God's Presence, which is everywhere, and yet remains directly above everything, is Christ's Eucharistic Presence.

Though Our Lord's body in its glorified condition has only one natural, spacial Presence in the universe, viz. heaven, at the same time God, in His omnipotence, has given it a supernatural, non-spacial power of presence, which it exerts at the same time with its natural spacial Presence. As the rule for this supernatural, non-spacial Presence is God's omnipotence, there is no limit to points of the universe at which it may exert itself simultaneously. This is what I call the majesty of the Eucharistic Presence.

It is no more a humiliation than the omnipresence of God; it is, on the contrary, a perfection of state too high for even angelic acumen.

That God should inhabit on high, and yet dwell in the lowest nature—this is the majesty of Divine Presence; it is first and greatest.

That the Son of man should have ascended bodily where He was first, and yet should be in every corner of the universe bodily—this is the majesty of the Eucharistic Presence; it is the second greatest and most merciful Presence marvel.

CHAPTER XXXVIII

THE BLOOD OF CHRIST

ALMIGHTY God has made man's salvation and sanctification depend on the pouring out of the blood of His only begotten Son. Our Lord's life, up to the shedding of His blood, was a life of immeasurable sanctity, a life of an infinite moral perfection. Yet it is not to any act of that wonderful career our Redemption and Sanctification are due.

The humility of His birth, the hidden prayer and obedience of His thirty years at Nazareth, the zeal and labour and bitterness of His public preaching did not win the salvation and redemption of mankind. We know, of course, that all those years of Our Lord's life were infinitely meritorious; but we know with less certainty in what manner those merits of the God-man benefit the human race; we know, however, that it is not through them we were bought back from the servitude of Satan. Our price, the price of our redemption, is essentially the precious blood of the unspotted Lamb.

The blood of God's Son poured out like water, the blood of God's Son drunk by man, absorbed by the higher nature of man—this and nothing else was to be our redemption and our sanctification.

In making the blood of His Son the price and vehicle of every grace, God has shown wonderful knowledge of the mysteries of human nature—if one could use these words with regard to One who has made human nature.

Our blood is our human individuality. We are what we are through the communication of the blood of our parents. Our far-reaching differences of temperament and power come from the blood that flows in our veins. It makes us of what nature we are : apt for good, or prone to evil.

Neither the philosopher nor the theologian can lay too much stress on the phenomena of heredity—phenomena that invariably point to the fact that it is man's blood that contains the germs of parental depravities or perfections.

In the blood of the Son of God we have a blood of absolute human purity—a blood that carries no germs of evil, but is filled, through the human laws of heredity, with every perfection because it is blood from an Immaculate Mother.

The blood of Our Lord is precious, primarily on account of Mary's spotlessness, through the immunity from all concupiscence, which was our Lady's privilege. That Our Lord's blood should have been endowed with absolute human purity we owe to Mary. Had she had the seeds of sin in her blood, the *fomes peccati*, Our Lord's blood might still have received purity from above; but it would not have had human purity, it would not have been precious as a human blood.

But now, thanks to Mary's spotlessness, human blood flowed in the veins of our Lord that came down from Adam, and had nothing in itself except what was purest and noblest in the human race from the beginning.

Besides this accumulation of human perfections, the blood of Our Lord was made still more precious through the indwelling of the Spirit of God. It had divine heredity besides human heredity. The Spirit of God had filled it with the fulness of Divine Life, when it was already precious as the product of Mary's noble life.

In this twofold heredity we have the key to the mystery of the Precious Blood; we know now why both its atoning and sanctifying power are infinite.

St. Paul, in one of his pregnant sentences, makes it easy for us to remember the whole theology of the Precious Blood. ' For if the blood of goats and oxen, and the ashes of an heifer being sprinkled, sanctify such as are defiled: How much more shall the blood of Christ, who by the Holy Ghost offered Himself unspotted unto God, cleanse our consciences from dead works, to serve the living God?'[1]

The blood unspotted, filled with the Holy Ghost, poured out through that very generosity communicated to it by the Holy Ghost, purifies the conscience, not externally, but internally by raising it, ennobling it—in one word, by making it serve the living God.

The blood of Our Lord is drunk by our soul in the mystery of the Holy Eucharist, is drunk by that highest and innermost part of ourselves, where spiritual temperament, or conscience, are to be found; and it gives to that part of our being, by a new kind of heredity, its own nobility; it makes us have God in our blood.

When you are in contact with a Catholic people, with Catholic multitudes (for masses are the best guide in these things), you find a refinement of thought, a depth of feeling in things spiritual, a keen insight into heavenly matters, which are painfully wanting in non-Catholic populations.

You ask yourself why this gulf between the mental states of two families of people, geographically and racially perhaps, so near. There is only one answer possible: It is in the blood—in the blood that is drunk by the Catholic people, that has been drunk by their fathers and their fathers' fathers.

[1] Heb. ix. 13, 14.

THE BLOOD OF CHRIST

The blood of our Lord, wherever it is found, must produce great confidence in God ; confidence in God is its primary and principal effect. Not only does it give us confidence through the belief that we have been bought at so great a price, but it gives confidence by a kind of heredity, a psychological transformation in the spirit that receives it. We become spiritually, supernaturally sanguine. We expect everything from God, precisely because we have in our veins that precious blood that makes the heart of the Son of God throb with unlimited confidence in the goodness of the Father.

CHAPTER XXXIX

THE OPTIMISM OF THE INCARNATION

THE fact alone of Hypostatic Union should turn the scales in favour of religious and theological optimism. How could mankind be a doomed race after the Personal Union of Divinity with one individual member of that race? How could our prospects be hopeless when we consider that man is God, and that God is man? if, with St. Thomas, I may be permitted to make use of these two convertible propositions in order to express the privilege conferred on humanity. The Godhead of Christ is a fact of infinitely greater reality than all the accumulated sinfulness of the human race. A race in which a Divine Person could be fittingly enshrined through a union such as is Hypostatic Union could not be radically bad to start with. It is true there is only one individual nature of that race that was thus united. All the same with God as his brother, man's future must be predominantly lightsome. By all the laws of thought, an infinitude of goodness, such as is the property of Christ's Personality, is

THE OPTIMISM OF THE INCARNATION

for the human race, which is Christ's race, a vastly more significant fact than that immense accumulation of moral deformities which are mankind's history. If mankind has, as we know it to have, spiritual enemies of a higher order and preternatural perverseness, one could hardly think of a more admirable way for them of wronging man than to blind him to the fact of that overtowering sanctity which is in Christ, and which can never have a corresponding moral evil, so to speak, of equal size.

But there is more than mere presence amongst us of a Brother who is a Personality of infinite perfection; He is not only a Presence that gladdens us by its glories, but He has come to us in the infinitude of His grace with wonderful determination to work at our salvation. He has come with infinite resolve to take away sin, to destroy death, to give life. 'Blotting out the handwriting of the decree that was against us, which was contrary to us. And he hath taken the same out of the way, fastening it to the cross; and despoiling the principalities and powers, he hath exposed them confidently in open shew, triumphing over them in himself.'[1]

Who would dare to accuse St. Paul of using hyperbolic language? Such a deed described by St. Paul as accomplished by the God-man changes for ever the mutual position of moral good and

[1] Col. ii. 14, 15.

moral evil. Mankind's moral good from the very fact of the Incarnation, as I have said already, is infinitely greater than mankind's guilt. All men put together could never commit sin that would be a dark spot as large in size as is that bright sun, Christ's sanctity. But there is more than that: the sin of man has been positively assailed by Christ; He has destroyed it in His own body, He has swallowed it like a poison, and though He died through it He found a higher life in His death.

We are all used from our childhood to expressions of that kind; all the same, we find it difficult to live in the serene optimism of the Epistles of St. Paul. After all, we say, souls are lost even now, and perhaps in large numbers. How can there be optimism with that dreadful terror? Is not every preacher at pains to inspire us with terror at the number of those that go to perdition? I have no opinion as to the relative numbers of the saved and the lost. Our Lord has warned us in the Gospels against the presumption that wants to look beyond the practical issues of spiritual life.

But if one thing is clear to me it is this: that such losses, whatever their number may be, could never take away one jot or tittle from that glorious optimism which is the Christian's birthright. I am sure of the fact that God became man and that He put infinite energy and sincerity into the work of man's salvation; of this I am sure with all the conviction of my Christian faith. If there are human beings that are lost, I feel certain that their loss is of such a description that it need not excite in me the least compassion: for I know that if their salvation had been possible it would have been accomplished by the redemption of Christ. I know that if there had been good will, such good will would have become an instrument of happiness in the hands of the God-man. Simple souls many times ask the question: How is it that the elect can be happy in heaven for all eternity, if there be a correspondingly long period of misery for other rational beings—the reprobate in hell? I know it is a difficult task to convince those good souls of the futility of reading their present kind feelings for every suffering beast into the spirit-state of eternity; one thing is certain: with that perfection of human nature which comes from consummate sanctity, the elect in heaven enjoy happiness that cannot be darkened one moment by the thought of the miseries of the reprobate. Reprobation, whatever it may be, is simply a thing that cannot excite compassion. If it could excite compassion, the whole universe would be at pains to find a remedy. It ought to be our first principle in thinking of reprobation that it is a state which is so absolutely the doing of the lost, without its being anybody else's fault, as to exclude compassion even from the heart of the Saviour.

So likewise with the sanctity of the Incarnation and the concomitant redemption. Its efficacy is not in the least diminished through the fact of the loss of men even under the new dispensation, and the possibility of souls being lost under the very shadow of the cross does not limit the extent of that constant truth expressed in the scriptures that Christ destroyed sin completely. It may be difficult for my finite mind to reconcile the two facts; but the fact of God's death on the cross is an infinite fact. It is the one fact which I am exhorted by every Christian authority to cherish and to keep before my eyes. I shall look at the world through that fact, and all other things must take up their position accordingly. To say that Christ's work of redemption is in any way a failure is downright blasphemy. We may say indeed that Christ failed during His mortal life to win the hearts of His enemies, but it could never be true to assert that the eternal loss of any human being could be a slur on the efficacy of the Grace of the cross.

There are strange aberrations in the minds of even good people, which no doubt come to those minds from their being too much the slaves of imagination and sentiment. It is just possible that even a holy man might have his spiritual life darkened through the thought of the loss of many, in spite of Christ's cross, or even perhaps through an abuse of Christ's grace. I should begin by telling him not to be more perfect than the saints in heaven, who cannot suffer simply because they see all things in the light of eternal truth. Eternal loss is not meant, and cannot be meant, to be an object of compassion precisely because it is irremediable; if it could be terminated and its termination could be hastened by our efforts, compassion would indeed be well employed, at least spiritual compassion; for when it is a question of mortal beings pitying spirit-beings, ordinary tenderness of heart would be a very bad guide. But let the holy man pour out his active mercies over people here on earth, who have it in their power not to go to that place of torment. Let him pity the souls of men because they do not make use of the graces whilst graces lie at their door. Such were Our Lord's compassions and sadnesses.

It may seem contradictory that one should be exhorted to have compassion on people who run towards their ruination when they have it in their power to run towards life eternal, and not to have compassion on them any more when they have actually fallen into eternal perdition. A reader might accuse me of being like a man whose heart is filled with distress because he sees a friend gambling away his family estate, and who adopts an attitude of supreme indifference towards the poor wretch when once he is in the workhouse. But the comparison is not fair. The human soul that leaves this life outside the grace of Christ no longer belongs to humanity; it no longer belongs even potentially to the mystical body of Christ; its severance from redeemed humanity is such that Christ Himself, who is the head of the human race, cannot own it any more.

We are all used to the beautiful expression that Christ is the head of the Church. St. Paul's theology is summed up in it.

St. Thomas Aquinas, however, goes one step farther, and declares Christ to be the head of all men. In question eight of the third part of the Summa, he shows how Christ is indeed the head of the Church, in virtue of an actual *influxus* of spiritual vitalities on His part into the souls and bodies of the baptised. But these considerations are followed by an article entitled *Utrum Christus sit caput omnium hominum*—' Whether Christ be the Head of all men.' I quote his own words; they are wonderfully liberal and generous. ' I say therefore that, speaking universally and taking in the whole duration of the world, Christ is the Head of all men. But this has various degrees. For He is first and mainly Head of those who are actually united to Him through (heavenly) glory.

' In the second place, He is the Head of those who are actually united to Him through charity. Thirdly, of those who are united through faith to Him. Fourthly, of those who are united to Him only

THE OPTIMISM OF THE INCARNATION 267

potentially (as a possibility), a potentiality not realised yet, but which is to be realised one day according to divine predestination. Fifthly, then, is He the Head of those who are united to Him merely potentially, according to a potentiality that is never to be realised: such are men who live in this world, but are not predestined to heaven. Such men, however, when they leave this life, cease absolutely to be members of Christ, because they are no longer endowed with the capability of being united to Christ.'

Reprobation is the only power that tears man away from the sweet possibilities of the Incarnation. The reprobate lacks the potentiality of being Christ's; he is of another world altogether.

Very wisely, and very generously, St. Thomas makes that wonderful potentiality consist in two things only: the power of Christ, and freedom of will on the part of man. 'Which potentiality is founded on two things: first indeed and chiefly, in the power of Christ that is sufficient for the salvation of the whole human race; then, in a secondary way, in the freedom of will.'[1]

[1] Ad 1 um.

CHAPTER XL

CHRIST THE HERO

THE fact of an individual human nature being united hypostatically with Divinity is a spiritual fact of the highest importance quite on its own merits. In other words, our spiritual life is raised up wonderfully not only through what Christ did and said and taught, but the fact of Christ, the fact of Hypostatic Union, makes us live, if we are but willing, in an entirely new world. How could we ever take a merely natural view of mankind if we are at all convinced that there has been a man who is God—God in the inexhaustible infinitude of meaning that is implied in the word 'God'?

The great ones of mankind have been benefactors not only through the things they did; but their very greatness as such is their best benefaction, because their intrinsic greatness raises the race and gives it a renewed consciousness of its excellency. Therein no doubt lies the charm of every great biography: a great man becomes easily the friend and the idol of many of more humble calibre to whom the external activities of the great man have practically been of no profit.

So with Christ: His being God, with all the excellencies and powers implied in the Hypostatic Union, His being so great is in itself and by itself mankind's best treasure. The world's teeming millions are not too big a crowd for One so elevated; He stands amongst them as distinctly cognisable as if He were alone; He is so great that the hubbub of endless worlds could never succeed in drowning the least whisper from His lips.

Hypostatic Union, with its infinitude of personal worth, becomes I might almost say a mathematically proportionate thing, if we consider that Christ is the one Person of whom every human individual to the end of the world might say with as much fulness and truthfulness as every other human creature: 'He is my ideal, He is my hero, He is my love.'

The sensation of the pilgrim who sits by the Lake of Galilee and says to himself with such absolute certainty, 'On these waters Christ sailed,' is no doubt a terrestrial embodiment of that much vaster thought that must fill the angelic mind when it looks at the human race. 'This is the race out of which there came God.'

No doubt there is a quickening of soul and body in Christ's faithful through Christ's grace that makes of that kind of hero-worship a unique thing, a life-giving thing, a kind of hero reproduction. Christ is our ideal indeed, but He is also our life. Yet, as an ideal and as a mere raising up of one human individual to an infinite altitude, Hypostatic Union ought to colour with optimism the whole human outlook.

To discard in practice the fact that we are dealing with creatures who by the very laws of their nature are the brothers of God, is the cruellest of all lapses of memory. However mean my neighbour may be, Christ's Personality is vast enough to reach out to him, just as the lowest animal may look at the sun. That some or even many human beings have a special kind of relationship with Christ, through their baptism, does not supersede the more elementary fact that all men are of the family of which God came.

It may even be said that Christ's activities, of whatever kind, in the world and on the world, are intended as means to win man to the practical realisation that He their God is amongst them.

CONCLUSION

IF the New Testament is to be taken literally, if its grammar, like the grammar of every great book, is the child of higher thinking, then we are happy people indeed. Then the primary and fundamental condition of our life is involvement in Christ's Divine and infinite Personality, instead of its being an action from a distance. We may not be able to understand how we are thus contained, though infinitude in Personality cannot mean anything short of infinitude of comprehension, infinitude of infolding, even to the least educated mind. St. Paul's *pleroma* and ' in Christ,' if taken literally, ought to change our views on the nature of our spiritual life not less radically than the Copernican theories of the world changed the world's astronomical views. Instead of Christ revolving round about us, to warm us with His grace, we move inside Him, inside His Personality, according to the New Testament view of spiritual life—at least with that portion of our spiritual life that is the very centre of spirituality. Or, pressing the comparison from the science of heavenly movement still further, with a view to illustrate that mutuality of indwelling spoken of elsewhere, the elect being in Christ and Christ being in the elect, let us say that as the all-pervading ether fills and infolds the planet and keeps it in the sun's plane, so likewise Christ through the infinitude of His Personality dwells in those that have their supernatural being in Him. 'And the glory which thou hast given me I have given to them, that they may be one, as we also are one. I in them, and thou in me, that they may be made perfect in one; and the world may know that thou hast sent me, and hast loved them, as thou hast also loved me.'[1] In the spiritual, in the mystical order of things we have here something greater, something newer than the revised astronomies of modern times, but something too that human thought is slow to grasp. No doubt the indwelling of the Father in the Son, and of the Son in the Father, becomes easily the delight of a mind prone to lofty speculation; most of us love to look at the immensities of heavenly wonders; the blue sky and the starlit firmament are the oldest joys known to man. None of us have any difficulties in giving literal meaning to words that convey such mutuality of indwelling. But we may think such words to be less obviously literal when it is our neighbour, our companion in Christ's faith, who is meant as being part of that

[1] St. John xvii. 22-23.

wondrous system of divine concentric circles. In the regions of the North Pole, no doubt, it may become difficult to realise that the earth moves in the plane of the sun.

But discarding all metaphor now, the glories of the Hypostatic Union are intensely human in their aim. Hypostatic Union is not a spiritual prodigy that appears in the heavens for its own sake: the blade, and the ear, and the ripe fruit, happy children and old men basking in the sunlight here on earth, make of the immensity of the sun-ball a quite proportionate means to an end. But here is my metaphor again. Quite simply, then, if my mind delights in the sublime verities of Hypostatic Union, whilst I regard and treat my brother as though he were not God's brother too, the great mystery is for me a barren marvel.

There is endless food for thought in the fact that the great mystery of God, the Incarnation, the secret hidden in God from the beginning, should be connected indissolubly with Simon the fisherman, and Mary the woman with the seven devils, and the woman who had five husbands, with a sixth one who was not hers, and Judas who loved the Master whom he betrayed. They are figures and types of the humanity which will be Christ's conquest. ' Now Jacob's well was there; Jesus therefore, being wearied with his journey, sat thus on the well. . . . There cometh a woman of Samaria to draw water.

... Jesus answered and said to her : If thou didst know the gift of God, and who is he that saith to thee, Give me to drink ; thou perhaps wouldest have asked of him, and he would have given thee living water. . . . And immediately his disciples came, and they wondered that he talked with the woman. Yet no man said : What seekest thou, or why talkest thou with her ?. . . . I have meat to eat which you know not. . . . My meat is to do the will of Him that sent me, that I may perfect His work. . . . Behold I say to you, Lift up your eyes, and see the countries, for they are white already to harvest.' [1]

Sun of Justice, Word Incarnate, Thine is the blade, Thine is the ear, Thine is the ripe corn in the ear. Grant me to love Thy harvest, for which Thou shinest in the heavens in the glory of Thy Hypostatic Union ; keep my feet from trampling on the rising blade, whilst my intellect gazes at Thy beauty in the blue firmament ; keep my hands from plucking ruthlessly the ear that is whitening, whilst I walk through life full of the rapturous thoughts of Thy being God. Make me to understand that Thou didst become Sun for the sake of the blade, that Thou seest the possibility of a true worshipper of the Father there where I harden my thoughts and turn away my eyes. May my mind return thanks to Thee for the delights of the thought that Thou art one

[1] St. John iv.

with the Father, by generously accepting my oneness with my brother in Thee, and let me pay for my glorious freedom to go in and to go out in the infinitude of Thy most sweet Personality by cheerfully accepting Thy great Law, O Thou most long-suffering of Friends—' Bear ye one another's burdens, and so you shall fulfil the law of Christ.'

The Mayflower Press, Plymouth, England. William Brendon & Son, Ltd.

Printed in the United States
104076LV00005B/187/A